Jesus, Pilate and Paul

Based upon the author's

"THE JEWS, JESUS AND CHRIST"

An Amazingly New Interpretation of the
Trial of Jesus under Pontius Pilate,
with a Study of Little Known
Facts in the Life of Paul
Before His Conversion

by

G. GEORGE FOX

ISAACS & COMPANY
Publishers and Booksellers
CHICAGO, 1955

This Printing is Dedicated to

DR. PRESTON BRADLEY

Outstanding Clergyman; Valiant Battler for Democracy and
Justice; Friend of the Friendless; Devoted to the
Highest Interests of our Country.

BOOKS BY DR. G. GEORGE FOX

JUDAISM, CHRISTIANITY AND THE MODERN SOCIAL IDEALS

THE JEWISH BIBLE AS RELIGION AND LITERATURE

NAZIISM AND DEMOCRACY

AN AMERICAN JEW SPEAKS

THE JEWS, JESUS AND CHRIST

Preface

The continued demand for my "The Jews, Jesus and Christ," which is now out of print, and the suggestions of some of its readers, among which were requests for an elucidation of some of the topics treated, have prompted me to revise and enlarge the subject-matter of the book. While the response to "The Jews, Jesus and Christ," was gratifying, I have decided to devote much more space to the trial of Jesus and to the teachings of Paul, and publish the work under the name of "Jesus, Pilate and Paul."

I have not given an extended bibliography. I have selected a few outstanding authorities, and named them in the notes. These can be the sources for a more extended bibliography for those who want to investigate the topics in greater detail. I am greatly heartened by the desire of many men and women who seek a better understanding of the subjects treated, in order to cultivate more friendly relations with those whose religious views are strange to them.

I want to acknowledge my thanks to Prof. Donald Riddle for his encouragement, to Rabbis Samuel Schwartz and Morris Teller, and to Rev. George A. Fowler for suggestions, and to my wife for her constant and unselfish help.

G. George Fox

Table of Contents

Introduction

It is well for any two religious groups to discover what is in common between them. This is unquestionably the most effective way—the best way—for individuals of two groups to understand one another's religion, and thus to dissipate whatever lack of appreciation or whatever prejudice may obtain.

The common ground between Judaism and Christianity is extensive, and the relationship between these two faiths is intimate. Not only did Christianity grow out of Judaism, but the daughter religion retained the prolific, beautiful and highly ethical and spiritual religious literature of the mother. And in Jesus the relationship was both intimate and creative; the religion of Jesus was Judaism. That fact alone demonstrates the debt of Christianity to Judaism.

Yet it is not easy to discover the common ground between Judaism and Christianity. It might be supposed that the shared element of sacred literature would lead to understanding. Usually, however, Moses, the Prophets, and the Writings are, to the Christian, the "Old Testament," a prelude to the ultimate, the New Testament. Christians usually study the Old Testament as Christian literature. Similarly, many adherents of Judaism find their Scripture sufficient, and seldom acquaint themselves with Christian writings.

Understanding the common elements of Judaism and Christianity which are represented in Jesus is particularly difficult. For Christians the task involves adequate acquaintance with and appreciation of the "late" Judaism, i. e., the legalistic elements associated with Ezra and his successors. For Jews the task requires acquaintance with both the literature and the history of Christianity. The difficulties tax the best efforts of scholars. Fortunately there have been Jewish and Christian scholars who have devoted themselves to efforts in these fields. One thinks of Claude G. Montefiore, or of Joseph Klausner, and of George F. Moore—representatives of many, of whom the larger number have come from Judaism.

More is needed. There is pressing need for many scholarly contributions by more specialists. But there is a crying need for work which, itself scholarly in method, standard, and content, addresses itself to nonspecialists in Judaism and in Christianity. Such a work is here presented. Its author and I are friends of many years' standing. We have spent many pleasant hours discussing matters treated in this book. I gladly testify to Dr. Fox's scholarship; his competence is apparent in what he has written. I bear witness to the quality and to the zeal of his religious life. He has been the spiritual leader of large congregations. He is devoted to his faith. A liberal—that is to say, a free—religious scholar, he knows and values the religion of Jesus and Jesus himself. He has a concern that liberal Jews and liberal Christians share with him what he has discovered. I also have that concern. Dr. Fox has done me the honor of saying that he has learned something from my books; I delight to regard him as my Rabbi, for I have learned from him. When I was working in the field of New Testament history and literature I perceived that I must know late Judaism. I saw that I could not learn all that I needed to know from books alone, but that I must learn by knowing Jewish people. It was here that my association with Dr. Fox was of inestimable value. For example, I learned something about the Passover from books, but I learned more from participating in a Passover Seder with Dr. Fox's congregation.

At that time I had a Jewish student in one of my classes. It was shocking to learn that he, a gentle, cultivated scholarly young man had as a boy been taunted with the epithet "Christ killer." So long as any Christian, by environmental or by whatever other stimulus, is ignorant of or ill disposed toward persons who are his spiritual kin, there is need for what Dr. Fox is here doing. He does it well. I am glad to recommend the present work to my co-religionists. I hope that they will respond to its messages and will propagate its point of view and its findings. Many will differ at one point or another. But Christians and Jews may unite in the basic credo: "The Lord, our Lord is one." Jews and Christians may be as one in recognizing that to love the Lord our God and our neighbor as ourselves, is the fulfillment of all Law— Torah and Gospel.

DONALD W. RIDDLE

The University of Illinois
Chicago Undergraduate Division

I.

The Teachings of Jesus

I.

THE GREAT UNCERTAINTY of the future and the gnawing insecurity with which the world is faced, have caused millions of men and women to seek hope and peace in the realm of religion. This has resulted in a growing good-will among individuals of different sects, and in a more friendly relationship between people of various religious points of view. There is much more free intermingling, for instance, between Jews and Christians than there used to be, and it is all to the good. But this increasing friendliness has brought to the fore basic questions which are being asked by both Jews and Christians. More and more frequently do we who participate in the larger social life of our land hear Christians ask: "What do Jews believe about Jesus Christ?" And many Jews ask: "What should be the attitude of Jews towards Jesus?" There is a growing belief on the part of many, that a knowledge of the answers would lead to more friendly relations between the two groups. It is felt that the misconception on the part of both Christians and Jews, of what the latter think of Jesus, and lack of the knowledge of the reason for the Jewish rejection of Jesus Christ, create animosities which induce suspicion and even hatred. The road to mutual understanding is blocked by ignorance or unfriendliness on both sides, and until these are cleared away, there cannot be that complete mutual good-will which so many so sincerely desire.

The attitude of the Jews towards Jesus the teacher, is a matter which does not interest Christians only. There are many Jews as well, who should be, and who want to be, informed about his life, his teachings, his death and his place in Jewish as well as in other modern religious life. The days that were darkened by distorted views and traditions regarding him, unfortunately are not over, and it is important that the historical facts about him be known to both Jews and Christians. Good-will is a two-way street, and only those who have divested themselves of misunderstanding and prejudice can travel it. There is a vast lack of knowledge regarding both the role that Jesus played in his day and what he taught, and only a clear understanding of his teachings and their meaning and his desires and aims, can destroy the wall of suspicion and misunderstanding that ignorance has erected.

This work is a study of the life, times and main teachings of the teacher of Nazareth, as well as an exposition and an explanation of the attitude of ancient and modern Jews towards the main teachings of Paul, the builder of Christianity, and the reasons for that attitude.

For nearly nineteen hundred years a conflict has been raging between the two great western mother and daughter religions and this disagreement has largely determined the attitude of their followers. That conflict had at times grown into much bitterness, and has resulted in indescribable suffering and even bestiality; and it has not yet been, in the main, satisfactorily resolved. But just as we find an evolutionary process in nature, in science, and in intellectual problems, so too, do we find it in the development of religious thought,[1] tho not all stages of this development are of a progressive nature. Just as we find reactionary periods in the history of political, social, and economic life, so are there periods of decline and even retrogression in the development of religions. The science of Comparative Religion teaches us that research, changing circumstances, new conditions of living and outmoded opinions have their effect both upon attitudes towards religious questions and upon interpretations of theological teachings.

Let us consider first the teachings of Jesus. The remarkable role that he has been made to play in our civilization, makes it difficult to believe that his life and death were so inconspicuous in his generation that his contemporaries with few exceptions took little or no notice of them. Yet this is the fact![2] He lived during one of the most turbulent periods of Jewish history. It was the period that followed the establishment of the Second Commonwealth and its final dissolution due to the quarrels of the later Maccabeans[3] and their Herodian descendants. The sons of Queen Salome Alexandra had made the tragic error of permitting the Roman Pompey to settle their dispute about who was to succeed their mother.[4]

In 63 before the Christian era he entered the Holy of Holies, and Roman domination began. A few years later (in 57) Alexander, the grandson of the late queen, made an attempt with some 11,000 men to regain a foothold in Judea. He was defeated. The next year another attempt was made, and that one failed. Two years later, 10,000 Jews were killed while trying again, and between 53 and 51 a large number were slaughtered while 30,000 were sold into slavery.

In a few years many thousands of Judeans had succumbed to the ravages of the wars with Rome. The exactions of the Romans became intolerable. The Temple was robbed several times, and the land and the people were literally being destroyed. Such was the inordinate greed of the Roman governors that if the Temple treasury failed to supply enough funds to satisfy their lust, special Temple taxes were levied. The Jews were helpless before the Roman terror. In 40 B.C.E., Herod, the son of Antipater the Idumean, was made king of Judea. He had married Mariamne, the daughter of Alexander of the Maccabean house, and Alexandra. In 37 he laid siege to Jerusalem which desired to be under the rule of the Maccabean Antigonus, for nearly two months and finally took it by storm. Josephus says of the victory:[5] "And now all parts of Jerusalem were full of those that were slain, by the rage of the Romans at the long duration of the siege. . . . so they were murdered continually in the narrow streets and in the houses by the crowds, and as they were flying to the Temple for shelter; and there was no pity taken of either infants or the aged, nor did they spare so much as the weaker sex. Nay, altho the king sent about and besought them to spare the people, yet nobody restrained their hand from slaughter, but as if they were a company of madmen, they fell upon persons of all ages without distinction."

The period of turbulence ceased during the reign of Herod. But he had incurred the hatred of the people he governed, and whose love he wanted, by his fawning to Rome, by his cruelty and greed,[6] and by his disregard and even contempt for their religious beliefs and customs. He yearned for fame and for the favor of Rome, and his love for vanity and public display led him to build palaces and cities which put heavy taxes and great financial burdens upon his subjects. His death, usually put at four years before the birth of Jesus, left Judea in great turmoil.

Herod's will provided that his son Archelaus should succeed him. But the people rebelled against him. Archelaus fought back, and the result was the slaughter of 3,000. Because Rome favored the Herodians, a number of Jewish anti-Roman disturbances took place in different parts of Palestine. These disorders were quelled; but in Jerusalem alone, 2,000 men were crucified. Archelaus was appointed ruler over Judea, but remained there only a few years when he was banished for political excesses. In the year 26, Pontius Pilate was appointed procurator of Judea.[7] He set about on a career of acquiring wealth, no matter at whose expense. He cared as little for the feelings of Jews as did most of his predecessors. He levied taxes and imposed burdens upon them. When the Judeans protested because he robbed the Temple, and the protest against this kind of action became too violent and troublesome, he sent his soldiers disguised as Judeans to mingle with the crowds and to attack them. Many were thus wounded and killed. The Jews were kept in constant terror of Pilate's acts which became more unbearable day by day. There was no appeal from his barbarity. The cowardice of the Judean aristocracy, the corruption of High Priests—favorites of Rome; the bitter hopelessness of the whole situation, brought forth ardent hopes for the Messiah, and any superiorly gifted individual could find followers if he acclaimed himself the Chosen One. Indeed, about the time of the rise of Jesus, several pseudo-saviors had already appeared. Many thousands of lives were lost and much blood was shed in these worthy messianic attempts to free Israel from Roman oppression. To bring about the Kingdom of God when the Roman Jewish world was in such deep suffering, was the obsession of many patriotic Jews, and the indwelling ambition of great and popular leaders.[8] No less a teacher than Rabbi Akiba, the greatest rabbi in his generation, living more than a century later, is said to have regarded Bar Kochba, the leader in the revolution against Hadrian, as the Messiah.

Pilate's abuses knew no bounds.[9] He was unscrupulous as well as treacherous. He used Temple funds for purposes which furthered his own plans. He was unconcerned about the murder of Jews, and Luke (13:1) mentions the Galileans "whose blood Pilate had mingled with their sacrifices." For ten years he added crime to crime. He showed his contempt for the religion of the people he governed; he spurned their sacred traditions. He sentenced to death men who were denied legal processes, and who had been tortured in submission. This denial of privileges which were held sacred by Jewish law and custom and the flaunting of contempt for the freedom which Jews enjoyed under their laws, drove them to distraction.[10] During these years the yearning for a Messiah that would overthrow Rome reached one of its highest points in the history of Israel. This was the same Pontius Pilate that crucified Jesus.

II.

It was at this time of national calamity that Jesus of Nazareth appeared. He was a man whose forebears were unknown except in the city of his youth where his father was a carpenter. The family had no special standing and the efforts of the Gospels to give Jesus a Davidic ancestry are not accepted as historical by most scholars. If the mortal father of Jesus had been a descendant of King David, something of honor and prestige would have been attached to the family.[1] Descendants of the Jewish nobility generally belonged to the Sadducean Party, of which the Temple priests were descendants and adherents. So far as is known, neither the ancestors of Mary the mother of Jesus, nor the family of Joseph his father, were Sadducees or descendants of noble blood. There is no historical record outside of the New Testament, whose writings are much later, that shows royal lineage. There is absolutely no contemporary record indicating such descent.[2] Jesus grew to young manhood in Nazareth without any special distinction, so far as contemporary records indicate. When near the age of thirty—authorities are not agreed—he started out for Jerusalem, the heart of Judea, to offer something of hope and comfort to his oppressed and disheartened brethren. The times were too serious and too dangerous for the men and women of Judea to take note of the doings of every inspired teacher. Nor could they have taken particular notice of the death of one, who, they could not have known, would some day be the most powerful influence in the history of western man.

It is often asked, "why was not Jesus accepted as the Messiah by his contemporaries," and "does it not seem reasonable to believe that the people of his own faith and generation should have been the first to acclaim him as the anointed of God?" But they did not. And the reason is, in short, that according to the records of his contemporary history, his birth, his activity and his death made little stir or impression upon them, because he did not fit into the accepted messianic patterns and qualifications.[3] There were many others who came to regard themselves as possible saviors, and thus commanded some attention until apprehended by the government and killed. We shall name some of them later.

From before the death of Herod and a number of years before the birth of Jesus, until the destruction of Jerusalem, there developed a passionate hope for a Messiah who would vanquish Rome, and restore Judea to peace and to her former glory. Isaiah the Prophet had set forth both the character of the Messiah and his times. He was to be a scion of the House of David who would restore the power and splendor of Judea as of yore, who would rule in justice, and bring about everlasting peace to both man and beast. Later tradition developed and extended the messianic concept. As a matter of fact, conceptions of the Messiah had been developing more widely from the time of John Hyrcanus (135-105 B.C.E.) to the days of Jesus, and helped to produce what is called the Apocalyptic Literature, in which there were varying descriptions of the Messiah and the messianic days.[4] Some of the apocalyptic books deal with a heavenly Messiah and a future world-era. Some teach the advent of an earthly savior who will initiate a time of peace and glory on earth. There were other conceptions also. But the terrors imposed by the Roman oppressor threw the emphasis upon the hope and the necessity for a realistic this-worldly release from their cruelties, and created a deep yearning for the loosening of Israel's bonds.[5] It is interesting to note in passing, that the great teacher Hillel, 50 B. C. E. to about 10 A.C.E. stated (Sanh. 98h), that there would never be a Messiah for Israel, since he had already come in the days of King Hezekiah in whose reign Isaiah prophesied. This opinion however, was not accepted by the Jewish people.

The Jewish Encyclopedia (Vol. 8, p. 509), quoting the Psalms of Solomon (Ps. XVII), written during the first century B.C.E., gives an excellent summary of the personality and the reign of the Messiah. He is designated as the "son of David". He "will first crush the unjust rulers and rid

Jerusalem of, and destroy, the impious heathen. Then he will gather the scattered ones of Israel, distribute them thru the land according to their tribes, and establish his own kingdom of peace and justice. No wicked person will be tolerated in his kingdom nor will foreigners be allowed to dwell there. He will subject the heathen nations to his rule, glorify the Lord before the whole world, and make Jerusalem pure and holy as of old, so that the nations will come from the ends of the earth to witness God's glory." The description of his righteous reign which follows, shows the influence of Isaiah XI. "Free from sin, strong in the divine fear, and filled with the spirit of God, of valor and of justice, he will tend the flock of the Lord faithfully, hold the higher officers in check, and make sinners cease by the power of his word, so that injustice and tyranny will not be practised in the land. He will not rely upon horses and warriors nor heap up gold and silver to wage war, nor keep armies. In God alone will he place his trust, and his strength will be in Him."

In general, the main features of this description of the Messiah were held by many of the contemporaries of Jesus.[6] Some of these qualifications applied to him. But as Roman oppression grew more brutal and the cruelty of the Romans more savage, the deep-seated yearning became more intense —and Jesus did not satisfy it. That the Jews had cause to expect a warrior-savior, is attested to by Josephus who mentions the "terrors of Pilate, his cruel deceptions, the barbarity of his orders to the soldiers, and his great injustice to the Judeans." Philo testifies that Pilate's administration was characterized by "corruption, robbery, violence and ill-treatment of the people, and continuous executions without even the form of a trial." [7]

To sum up the messianic beliefs: There were those who believed that the Messiah would be a mortal leader, a scion of the House of David, whose time was surely approaching and who, with upheld sword would repeat the miracles of the Maccabean victors. Others thought of the Messiah as a sort of other-wordly, semi-divine creature, a sort of [8] celestial being created before the world was created, who would come to judge mankind, the righteous and the sinners, even the demons, and who would be the savior of the righteous for the Kingdom of God on earth, which his presence would usher in. They were in the minority. But the more practical hoped for a messianic leader who would first deliver them from Roman rule, and then would establish their country as the home of justice and peace and mercy—the locale of God's Kingdom on Earth. They believed passionately that when the Redeemer would come and wrest the land from Edom—their favorite appellation for Rome—the words of Isaiah (Ch. 2:3) would be realized: "For from Zion shall go forth the Law (the Torah), and the word of the Lord from Jerusalem."

Jesus appeared probably about 29 of the Common Era. After his baptism and the death of John the Baptist, he returned to Nazareth where many scholars think he was born. Like most of the Galileans he looked forward to the advent of the Messiah who was to free Israel from the Roman

23

yoke. His baptism by John who believed himself to be the forerunner of the Messiah, no doubt strengthened the belief of Jesus in the hope. In the meantime, John was killed. Now that he was no more, was the hope in a savior to disappear? That could not be. The meaning of the prophecies, the predictions of the coming of a Messiah in the apocalyptic traditions, the very bitterness of the Judean sufferings, and the apparent hopelessness of the future for their own bettering their condition, all combined to dismiss the thought that even the death of John destroyed the hope of a savior. Jesus, whose very name means "savior," was troubled by the times. When John had proclaimed himself the forerunner of one "whose shoes I am not worthy to bear," and "I have need to be baptized of thee" (Mt. 3:11, 14), [9]Jesus could have assumed that he doubtless was the one predicted by the Baptist, if the Gospel story is to be believed.

III.

Shortly after this, Jesus began to preach. The burden of his message was "repent, for the Kingdom of Heaven is at hand." (Mk. 1:14). He traveled about—"teaching in synagogs, preaching the gospel of the kingdom, and healing all manner of disease among the people. (Mt. 4:23). Soon his "fame spread throughout all of Syria, and they brought him all sick people that were taken with diverse diseases and torments, and those which were possessed with devils, and

24

those which were lunatic, and that had palsy; and he healed them." (Mt. 4:24). It is easy to understand that as his reputation spread, Jewish multitudes from all over Judea followed him. As his name became better known, and as his following increased, his consciousness of his messiahship must have deepened. Please note that those who followed him and were served by him, were his own people who understood and spoke his language, not non-Jews as many today think. This verse is more New Testament evidence that he was not rejected by his own people; rather does it indicate that he was accepted as a teacher and healer.

As these months passed, the peoples' yearning for release from the trials imposed by the Romans became more poignant. The necessity for a King-Messiah who could lead Israel to victory over the detested Romans became more acute. Roman cruelty had struck deepest terror and despair into the hearts of the Jews. The Sadducean priesthood to which they looked for some relief, was largely corrupted by the Romans. No moment was safe from disaster and bloodshed. God seemed to have forgotten His people, to have forsaken the Children of Abraham. Daily the Messiah was expected. Anxiously news of his appearance was awaited.

More than a year had now passed since the name of Joshua (Jesus) first became known. Multitudes heard him; his teachings spread also among the Pharisees. A few questioned his interpretations; some doubted his powers. But the masses who heard him apparently found nothing contrary to their Jewish heritage. His enthusiasm and his concern for the "lost sheep of the House of Israel," (Mt. 10:6); his earnest-

25

ness, his use of the parable which he had learned from his teachers in his youth, and his association with the "sinners and publicans" because he believed in the truth of the statement later expressed by the words "although he has sinned, he is still an Israelite,"—all of these attitudes and teachings helped to attract to him the people who heard him, that is, his brethren of the House of Israel. If the Gospels are correct, the Jewish masses accepted Jesus as a teacher and as a healer, wholeheartedly and enthusiastically. (Mt. 21:8-11; Mk. 11:9-10; Lk. 19: 37-8).

We must not undervalue the popularity or the intensity of the Judean belief in the coming of the Messiah. The concept expressed the most fervent hopes for peace for the individual and the nation, and later the world. The word Messiah—meshiach, the anointed of God—in Hebrew—tho applied at first only to the one chosen king, became the symbol of the highest hopes for individual and national salvation. The word coined at a time of national distress by the prophetic hope for political salvation, was preserved and modified by whatever circumstances were created by historical changes that affected the destiny of Israel. As time went on, the individual-national ideal became a universal hope and ideal, and the promise of God's providence in bringing about that universal peace which the prophets visioned, and which the apocalyptists developed with a piety and a picturesqueness that gave courage and hope in times of the nation's deepest discouragement.

Whether the Messiah was to be the liberator who was to establish again the rule of David and who, according to the

Second Psalm would "break them (the nations) with a rod of iron, and dash them to pieces like a potter's vessel," or whether he was to be a mystical spiritual being "coming on the clouds," made little difference. The bitter plight under the Roman persecutions melted these different conceptions into an intense hope that something would happen, perhaps even a miracle, that would release Israel, and institute the approach of the hoped-for age beginning with the fall of, or the destruction of Edom—that is Rome—and the creation of the longed-for day of peace.

But neither the life nor the death of Jesus brought the messianic era about. He did not bring freedom to the stricken land, neither as a man of war nor as the "Prince of Peace," nor as the "wonderful counsellor," nor as a divine hero, "coming upon the clouds." The Romans were not discomfitted and conquered. Oppression did not cease; peace either in Judea or in the world was not established, and life was dark and oppressively dreary for Israel. The prophetic vision of Isaiah (Ch. XI) which gave birth to the messianic conception, was not realized. The ethical teachings that Jesus uttered were accepted by the multitudes that heard him—but what Israel needed at this time more than a prophet of the spirit, was a hero of Davidic stature. This, Jesus was not—and because he did not fulfill the conditions under which the Messiah was expected, he was not accepted by his people in his day, nor is he accepted by Jews today.

There were a number of [1] Jewish patriots called Pseudo-Messiahs who appeared in the first century before and after the destruction of the Temple. Among them were, according to historians Josephus and Graetz,[2] Simon, a slave of Herod; Athronges, Theudas, and an "unknown" Egyptian. Another whom Josephus called only "imposter," promised the people deliverance if they would follow him. Both Theudas and the "imposter" were killed by the Romans, while another called the "Egyptian prophet," escaped. One of the best known of those who came forward as saviors of their people was Judas the Galilean, the son of Hezekiah, who led a force to protect the Temple, but was overwhelmed. Another was John of Giscala. It was during this restless period that John the Baptist was executed, more because Herod Antipas, who at this time ruled Judea, feared a rebellion than that he wanted to please Salome.

The attitude of the Jews of Jesus' day towards him, if judged by the Gospels with the exception of a few unexplained passages, was as we have seen, a friendly one.[2] His disciples were Jews; his close friends were Jews; the majority of the lame and the halt who were brought to him were Jews; the "great multitudes of people from Galilee, Decapolis—a name applied to the League of Ten Cities mainly east of the Jordan River—and Jerusalem, and people of Judea and beyond the Jordan" who followed him, were Jews. (Mt. 21:8-11). Very few besides the Jews understood Aramaic, the language of Jesus. Matthew the tax-gatherer was a Jew; Simon the leper was a Jew; Mary Magdalene was Jewish as was Joseph of Arimathea; Jairus was a Jew; Lazarus was a Jew, and all of the disciples were Jews! The mul-

28

titudes that went before him and followed him, crying "Hosana to the son of David" were Jews. (Mt. 21:9 and similar passages). On the basis of these Gospel narratives, the Jews of Jesus' day certainly had no ill-feeling against him. On the contrary, some thought him to be the "one looked-for." But Judeans as a whole, were expecting help thru a military as well as a spiritual hero, who would embody within himself the messianic qualifications enumerated in Isaiah: "For unto us a child is born, to us a son is given; and the government will be upon his shoulder, and his name is called Wonderful Counselor, Mighty God, Everlasting Father, Prince of Peace. Of the increase of his government and of peace there will be no end. Upon the throne of David and over his kingdom to establish it, and to uphold it with justice and righteousness from this time forth and for evermore. The zeal of the Lord of Hosts will do this." (Is. 9:6-7).

"And there shall come forth a shoot out of the stock of
　　Jesse (the father of David),
And a twig shall grow forth out of his roots.
And the spirit of the Lord shall rest upon him,
The spirit of wisdom and understanding,
The spirit of counsel and might,
The spirit of knowledge and of the fear of the Lord.
And his delight shall be in the fear of the Lord,
And he shall not judge after the sight of his eyes,
Neither decide after the hearing of his ears;
But with righteousness shall he judge the poor,
And decide with equity for the meek of the land;
And he shall smite the land with the rod of his mouth,

And with the breath of the lips shall he slay the wicked.
And righteousness shall be the girdle of his loins
And faithfulness the girdle of his reins.
And the wolf shall dwell with the lamb,
And the leopard shall lie down with the kid;
And the calf and the young lion and the fatling together;
And a little child shall lead them.
And the cow and the bear shall feed,
Their young ones shall lie down together;
And the lion shall eat straw like the ox.
And the suckling child shall play on the hole of the asp,
And the weaned child shall put his hand on the basilisk's
    den,
They shall not hurt nor destroy in all My holy mountain.
For the earth shall be full of the knowledge of the Lord,
As the waters cover the sea (Is. 11:1-9, 10, 12-13).
And it shall come to pass in that day,
That the root of Jesse that standeth for an ensign of the
    people,
Unto him shall the nations seek.

* * * * *

And He will set up an ensign for the nations,
And will assemble the dispersed of Israel,
And gather together the scattered of Judah
From the four corners of the earth.
The envy also of Ephraim shall depart.
And they that harass Judah shall be cut off.

* * * * *

And they shall fly down upon the shoulder of the Philis-
    tines on the West;
Together they shall spoil the children of the East;
They shall put forth their hands upon Edom and Moab;
And the children of Ammon shall obey them."

Add to this, the verses in the second chapter of Isaiah,
stated again almost verbatim in the fourth Micah, and it
becomes quite obvious that the messianic day had not yet
arrived in Judea. The verses in Micah (4:1-4), read as
follows:

"But in the end of days it shall come to pass,
That the mountain of the Lord's house shall be established
    as the top of the mountains,
And it shall be exalted above the hills;
And peoples shall flow into it.
And many nations shall go and say: "Come ye and let
    us go up to the mountain of the Lord,
And to the house of the God of Jacob;
And He will teach us of His ways,
And we will walk in His paths;
For out of Zion shall go forth the Law,
And the word of the Lord from Jerusalem;
And He shall judge between many peoples,
And shall decide concerning mighty nations afar off;
And they shall beat their swords into ploughshares,
And their spears into pruning hooks;
Nation shall not lift up sword against nation,
Neither shall they learn war any more;

But they shall sit every man under his vine and under
his fig-tree
And none shall make them afraid;
For the mouth of the Lord of hosts hath spoken."

The fact that the tribulations of the days of Jesus continued, and in no wise indicated that the peace that was
expected was being ushered in by a Messiah; the fact that
Jesus was a gentle teacher rather than a man of war; the
increasing terrors of Rome and the apparent inability of
any ordinary Jewish leader to stop them; the fact that several arose who thought that they were the Messiahs, but
were apprehended by the Romans and killed—and the fact
that there was no sign from heaven to indicate that he was
the chosen of God who would come riding upon the clouds,
as was predicted in some of the Hassidean and Apocalyptic
books—all these circumstances conspired to make impossible the acceptance of Jesus as the Messiah foretold in the
Jewish tradition.[3]

The attitude towards Jesus of most of his contemporaries,
and that of the next generation after him, was one of indifference. The people who had known him and regarded him
as their Messiah formed a small party and only later became known as the first "Christians." But there was no
unfriendliness between these and other Jews in the beginning. Some members of a family could very well have believed in him, while others did not. Families could be
divided so that some members, for instance, would be followers of the school of Hillel, others of that of Shammai.

There was no question then as to the right or privilege of being a follower either of Jesus, who was just another teacher in the House of Israel, or of some other religious teacher. In the meantime what became the contents of the Gospels was in process of formation. Stories of the life and activities of Jesus were being circulated by his followers, and were later recorded.[4] There was a great deal of missionary activity on the part of his disciples—even before the journeys of Paul. By the year 67, when Vespasian decided to subdue Judea, there was a well-defined line of demarcation between those who were the followers of the Jesus-Messiah group and the rest of the Judeans, because the former were refusing to cooperate with the Judeans in the Roman war. The stories which were to be incorporated in the Gospels were beginning to have their effect.[5]

IV.

It is thought by some biblical critics that the first three Gospels—Matthew, Mark and Luke—could have been written in Hebrew or Aramaic.[1] The earliest Gospel was produced in Rome about 70 A.C.E. This is regarded as being the Gospel of Mark. The other three are later. Some place completion of the Gospels much later. Most scholars agree that these records did not assume a canonical or privileged character until the second half of the second century, and some place the final redaction of the Gospels as late as 170 of the Christian Era. Jesus did not write one word or syllable of what we now call the New Testament. Caspar Rene Gregory, one of the greatest of the New Testament scholars, wrote in his great book, "Canon and Text of the New Testament"[2]: "So far as we know, Jesus left no writings, no notes behind him. We do not read that he ever told anyone to take down his words so as to give them to others, in white and black. We are not told that he wrote or dictated even a letter." Dr. James Moffatt, in his [3] "Introduction to the Literature of the New Testament," tells us: "There is abundant evidence that the men and women who circulated the stories about Jesus did not hesitate to add a detail here and there, or change a phrase of a thought here and there. The copyists were not always correct in their manuscripts, and added or deleted such matter as they deemed harmful to their cause. For it must not be forgotten that the gospel-documents were to a very large extent propaganda material. Tracts and letters were written in the names of the Apostles and Paul to give them authority, and as early as the second half of the second century the authenticity of the then New Testament writings was so much in doubt, that Marcion, a Christian of that day, was accused of falsifying the Gospel. A number of copies of the Gospels existed, but there was widespread diversity among them." Indeed there is still diversity among the Gospels!

Charles Guignebert, regarded by many as the most eminent French historian of the Christian Religion, tells us in his [4] "Christianity, Past and Present": "It was therefore, from elements that were heterogeneous and very unequal in value

that the tradition (paradosis) was fashioned which the believers in the first generation after Christ accepted as the
authentic history of the Master. It was only after those be-
longing to the first generation were in their graves that this
disappearance of the direct witnesses of Jesus, one after
another, gave rise to doubts as to the imminence of the
expected coming of the Lord. Then it was that the more
prudent Christians deemed it expedient to commit to writing the recollections which oral tradition was reputed to
have preserved.

"First to be formed, probably, were little books of memo-
randa in which each writer collected what he deemed especially interesting; connected sayings attributed to the Master;
accounts of episodes in his life which were characteristic
or edifying; descriptions of the 'signs' that is, miracles
which he had performed to confound the incredulous. Nobody troubled about what we term historical exactitude,
which presumes scruples unknown or indifferent to men of
an ardent faith, who are therefore as devoid as possible of
a critical spirit; on the other hand, each one aimed at estab-
lishing the soundness of the Christian hopes, at convincing
the doubters and edifying the believers. These little books
constituted the ancient sources of the Gospels."

Prof. Case has this to say regarding the historicity of the
Gospels:[5]

"We have to admit that the New Testament may contain
features created by the pious fancy of early believers, hence
a request for more specific proof that the earthly figure of
Jesus is not a mere product of this interest in interpretation,

is not out of place. The obscurity of Christian beginnings makes our task a difficult one. While there is ample evidence that the new religion was in existence about the close of the first century after Christ, there is no contemporary account of its beginnings, much less an account of its alleged founder. He left no written record of his teaching, and none of the New Testament writings can be assigned with absolute certainty to the pen of a personal disciple of Jesus. . . . It is now well-known that the literature which purports to narrate the story of Jesus' career does not in its present form come from the first generation of Christians."

In their exhaustive study entitled "The New Testament Life and Literature", Riddle and Hutson say among other things (Ch. XIV): "The Gospels were the books of the early church. They represent collections of materials which the early evangelists found useful for religious edification. Gospels were produced in response to felt religious needs within the developing communities; they reflect at the same time the traditions about the earthly Jesus and the interpretations which the early preachers made concerning him. It was the activity of the church which caused them to be written; they were the church's early books.

"A cursory examination of the literary character of the Gospels brings the conclusion that the materials spring from strata of folk-activity. A first reading of any one of the synoptic Gospels informs the analytical mind that the sermons, the old stories, the parables, the sayings, the miracle tales, and the legends represent collections from the life of a people. They did not originate in the mind of one creative author. A second conclusion is also inescapable: the primary concern of all this literature is religious motivation and indoctrination."

The authors illustrate these points by a thorough examination of the Gospel of Mark, and state (p. 156): "The careful reader will perceive that many statements within the Gospel of Mark show that the work was not intended for a Palestine reading public. Palestine coinage must be explained to the reader in the parable of the widow's lepta (Mk. 12:42: "two mites which make a farthing"). The season at which the Jewish Passover is celebrated is unknown to those who will read the Gospel (Mk. 11:13). The customs of the Pharisees are not understood: some of the ceremonial observations are cited. (Mk. 7:3-4). Aramaic expressions are not understood by the intended readers"; tho Aramaic was the language in daily use; Aramaic words in several verses had to be explained. (Mk. 5:41; 7:34). "These explanations of customs and language familiar in Palestine indicate that the Gospel was intended for a gentile reading public," and attests to its production as at least 70 years after Jesus' birth.

Pierre van Paassen, has this to say in his "Why Jesus Died" (p. 139): "The New Testament story is not pure invention. The gospel writers are not frauds. But they are not historians either. The accounts they give are not historic facts. The gospels we know are half-myth, half-fact, creedal affirmations, allegories, liturgical citations and material for edification of the faithful in which elements and fragments of objective, historic truth are mixed with embellishments, miracles, fantasy and mythology."

By the time of the Bar Kochba revolution in 132 of the Christian Era, [6] the separation between Jews and the followers of Jesus was complete. As a matter of fact, his disciples by that time definitely called "Christians," had withdrawn completely from the Jewish community, and directed their missionary efforts very largely to the Gentiles and to the Jews outside of Palestine. The Synoptic Gospels with their accusations against the Pharisees, and the Fourth Gospel with its general unfriendliness to the Jews, were doing their work. Where in the days of Jesus there was no ill-feeling against him and the Apostles on the part of the Jews, or ill-feeling against the Jews on the part of Jesus and his immediate followers, later this relationship was sharply and pointedly changed. Before the Roman war, according to George Foot Moore in his [7] "Judaism," "the disciples of Jesus of Nazareth had been a conventicle within the synagog, rather than a sect. The Jews had no doctrine about the Messiah invested with the sanction of orthodoxy; and on the fundamental articles of Judaism, the unity of God, his peculiar relation to Israel, the revelation of his character, will and purpose in Scripture, the Nazarenes were as sound as any Jew could be. It was more than two generations later, when the growth of Christianity had begun to engender feelings against the Jews because of the spread of Gospel stories and the teachings of Paul that some rabbis began to utter hostile utterances against it. There were the defensive retorts to the challenges in the Gospels and some Epistles, particularly to the Gospel of John which is strongly anti-Jewish." But these utterances were few and far between, and increased only in proportion to the number of church decrees which were later adopted and which resulted in the persecution of the Jews by the Church. James Parkes,[8] one of the latest authorities in this field, asserts in his "The Conflict of the Church and the Synagog": "No literature has survived, and it is doubtful if any ever existed, in which Jews set in writing their replies to the challenge of the Christians. At most, this or that paragraph in the Talmud may have been uttered with the Christian doctrine, and the reply to it in the mind of the rabbi." This seems to bear out the statement of G. F. Moore that "later controversy was with the Catholic Christians."

That later Jewry reciprocated the unfriendliness of the Christians is not to be wondered at. There was no reason why the Jews should not resent the accusations and the persecutions of the Church. As a matter of fact, until the fourth century,[9] and before the Church took its inimical stand, the friendliest relations existed in many communities outside of Palestine between Jews and Christians. But as early as the beginning of that time, in the year 305, the Council of Elvira composed of bishops of the larger Christian cities, decreed laws which prohibited Christians from living with Jews, from eating in their company, or having their fields blessed by them,[10] on pain of excommunication. The Jews were stigmatized as an "immoral, profligate, godless sect," which ought to be exterminated from the face of the earth.

The Emperor Constantine had a church council called at Nicea, in 320, consisting of several hundred bishops and priests with himself at the head. It was at this council that the last thread that connected Judaism with Christianity was cut. Heretofore, Easter and Passover were celebrated simultaneously, on the days set by the Judean Sanhedrin. This was changed to another day "for it is unbecoming beyond measure that on the holiest of festivals, we should follow the custom of the Jews. Henceforward, let us have nothing in common with this odious people; our Saviour has shown us another path. It would indeed be absurd if the Jews were able to boast that we are not in a position to celebrate the Passover without the aid of their rules." The historian, H. Graetz,[11] cites these statements as having been made at the Council of Nicea, and attributed to the Emperor Constantine.

Later at the Council of Laodicea, in the second half of the fourth century, Christians were forbidden to eat with Jews, to take part in any of their ceremonies or festivities, and above all to observe their sabbaths. In 339 under Emperor Constantine the son of Constantine the Great, a law was passed punishing with banishment or death any Jew who converted his slave to Judaism. The Jews were forbidden to keep Christian slaves, and marriages between Christians and Jews were made punishable offenses. The persecution of the Jews continued thruout these ages. In the Roman Empire, Spain, Portugal, France, Italy, England, Germany, Poland, Russia—in every country where Jews lived with the exception of Holland, the Church pursued them until the names of Jesus Christ and Christianity became the omens and the symbols of terror to them. The Cross was a sign of desperation and death, and the name of the Christian Saviour was the harbinger of inhuman ferocity. The New Testament was a closed and a proscribed book, and even the Jewish scholars who consulted it, did so largely as a dire necessity because they were forced into religious disputations with Christians or renegade Jews, by the Christian authorities.[12] The various means of punishment meted out to the sons of the House of Jacob by ecclesiastical and political dignitaries, from the enforced attendance at church on certain festivals to the auto-da-fe—the act of faith resulting in death by fire—strain the imagination and arouse the deepest resentment![13] It is no wonder that for centuries, even the mention of Jesus Christ, the Cross, and the Church evoked the strongest disgust and fear from the hearts of the Children of Israel.

In those Jewish circles which have felt the heels of the Christian persecutors in Europe, and particularly among those who still remember the east-European pogroms and massacres, there is still a feeling of unfriendliness towards the kind of Christianity which permitted its followers to continue the persecutions of the Dark Ages in the name of the Savior. The bitter hatred shown by worshippers of Jesus who vented their ire against the "Christ killers," was reciprocated by a similar hatred for the daughter religion and its Messiah. Time, however, has changed this feeling for most of the civilized world. The rise of humanitarianism has lessened the hurt of the wounds so often suffered by the Jews, and has tempered the hate induced by the story of the crucifixion. The spread of democratic ideals and the immortal teachings of the Declaration of Independence and the Constitution, have put our country in the forefront of the builders of a world of the Brotherhood of Man in the Fatherhood of God. The growth of liberal thinking beginning in the political area, as reflected in the American Revolution first and then the French Revolution, has extended to the religious. Christian men and women, under the aegis of democratic ideals and with the impetus of fair-play, have taken renewed interest in the study of the Scriptures. Likewise the pages of the New Testament formerly known only to some Jewish scholars have become the objects of study among many Jews. As they dig deeper into the history of Jesus and his time, they begin to understand that it was the fanatic followers of Jesus, not he, who were the cause of Israel's woes. They have begun to evaluate the terrible injustices which had been heaped upon them, in terms of ignorance and hatred on the part of the adherents of the dominant religion, rather than in terms of the teachings of its Messiah. There dawned upon them the consciousness that, though the tragedy of Jewish history has been the historic misunderstanding by the Church of the Jewishness of its own "Founder," he was not to be blamed for that vicious error. And as the liberal Jew began to emerge from the darkness of his fear and hate, so too, did the liberal Christian begin to get out from under the shadows of his horrid prejudices against the Jews, and away from the evils planned and carried out by churchmen.

The educated Jew of today has emancipated himself from his forebears' attitude towards Jesus, just as the liberal Christian has freed himself from the un-Christian feelings of his fathers towards the Jews. Unfortunately there is yet a great deal to be accomplished in this direction. But speaking for the Jews, I think fairness compels one to say that they have gone further towards a friendly appreciation of Jesus and the cultivation of interfaith good-will and understanding than his followers have come in their friendly attitude towards the Jews.

V.

I believe that it is universally agreed that no professing Jew can accept Jesus as the divine son of God, and as the "only begotten Son" of the New Testament Gospels. This conception is contrary to the basic belief of Judaism, namely, that there is but one God, one Creator indivisible, incorporeal, spiritual and eternal, the Father of all humankind. The God of Israel is not a substance that He can divide Himself or be divided. He is a spirit which fills the world and has no form. No conception of Him, according to Jewish teachings, can fit the Apostolic Creed, which reads: "I believe . . . in Christ Jesus, His only begotten Son, our Lord, who was born of the Holy Ghost and the Virgin Mary, who was crucified under

Pontius Pilate and was buried, on the third day rose from the dead, ascended into Heaven, sitteth at the right hand of the Father, whence He shall come to judge the living and the dead." Nor can it fit into the Nicene Creed, a part of which reads as follows: "We believe . . . in one Lord, Jesus Christ, the son of God, begotten of the Father, only begotten, that is of the substance of the Father, God of God, Light of Light, very God of very God, begotten not made of one substance with the Father, by whom all things are made, both those in heaven and those on earth, who for us men and for our salvation came down and was made flesh, and lived as man among men, suffered and rose the third day, ascended into heaven, is coming to judge the quick and the dead." One who professes the religion of Judaism, cannot under any circumstances accept the idea of a triune God,[1] that is a God who is "Father, Son and Holy Ghost," all in one. According to Judaism, the conception of Jesus Christ as the son of God and therefore of divine begetting, simply cannot be valid. According to the Scriptures, we are all the children of God, and God cannot divide Himself into a divine and a human substance—into a formless spirit and a human form.

Nor can Judaism accept the doctrine of Jesus Christ as the redeemer of mankind, in this world or in the next. Judaism has no doctrine which teaches redemption from sin either in this world or in the future world by the sacrifice of a human offering—or thru the blood of a human being. It is true that there were sacrificial offerings during the existence of the Temple. But that any human being could be used in the place of a lamb or of any other animal, and thus become the redemption-sacrifice from sin, is a thought that is foreign to Judaism and is condemned by Scripture. (II Kgs. 16:3). Altho the idea of original sin was not entirely absent in Judaism, it never occupied the place that it had and has in Christian theology. It is contrary to Jewish teaching to believe that a redeemer or savior—whether it be a god or man—can take upon himself the guilt of someone else's sin, by having his life sacrificed!

Dr. K. Kohler, the most eminent of American Jewish theologians, wrote in his "Jewish Theology,":[2] "From the very beginning, no Jewish doctrine was so firmly proclaimed and so heroically defended as the belief in the One and Only God. However slowly the people learned that there could be no gods besides the One God, and that consequently all pagan deities were but "naught and vanity," the Judaism of the Torah starts with the proclamation of the only One, and later Judaism marches thru the nations and ages of history with a never-silent protest against polytheism of every kind, against every division of the Godhead into parts, powers or persons. . . . Under all conditions, the doctrine of unity remained free from outward compulsion and full of intrinsic vigor and freshness. . . . This is Maimonides' statement of the unity: 'God is one; that is, He is unlike any other unit, whether made one in point of numbers or species, or by virtue of composition, separation, and simplification. He is one in Himself, there being no multiplicity in Him. His unity is beyond all definition.' Ibn Gabirol in his 'Crown of Royalty', puts the same thought into poetic form: 'One art

Thou; the wise wonder at the mystery of Thy unity, not knowing what it is. One art Thou; not like the one of dimension or number, as neither addition nor change, neither attribute nor quality affects Thy being. . . . Thou are God, and there is no distinction between Thy unity, Thy eternity and Thy being'." "I am the Lord, and there is none else; beside Me there is no God." (Is. 45:5).

M. Friedlander, the celebrated English Jewish theologian, said in his "The Jewish Religion":[3] "The Jewish doctrine of the Unity of God does not admit any kind of dualism in the Divine Being, and therefore rejects the existence of Divine Attributes as distinct from God Himself. He is One, simple and indivisible. The Creator is One, and there is no other oneness like His in any way. The Unity of God is the creed which the Jews have always proclaimed by word of mouth, to which they have given expression through their literature, and for which they have willingly sacrificed their lives as martyrs."

Judaism, therefore, does not believe in the theory of a redeemer such as is understood by the meaning of the statement in the Gospel of John: "The next day John seeth Jesus coming unto him and saith, "behold, the Lamb of God, which taketh away the sin of the world." (Jn. 1:29). As used originally in the Old Testament the word redeemer meant "blood redeemer or avenger" of the death of a kinsman. In the prophetic and later literature, the word is always applied to God. There is some Christian controversy as to the exact meaning of the word in Job (19:12), "I know that my redeemer liveth." Judaism applies this to God. The Pauline doctrine that thru his blood Jesus obtained eternal redemption for mankind (Hebrews 9:12) and similar passages, has no place in the Jewish religion.[4] When in the earlier life of Israel the word redeemer referred to the avenger of the murder of one's kin, this avenger-redeemer shed the blood of the killer, but never gave his own as Jesus is alleged by the Gospels and Paul to have done. The blood-sacrifices which were offered in the Temple had no reference at all or at any time to the redemption of sin after death. In the Prophets and in the Psalms, the word redeemer applies to God, as is indicated by the following passages:

Fear not, thou worm Jacob, and ye men of Israel, I help thee, saith the Lord, and thy Redeemer, the Holy One of Israel. (Is. 41:14).

And all flesh shall know that I the Lord am thy Savior and thy Redeemer, the mighty One of Jacob. (Is. 49:26).

Our Redeemer, the Holy One of Israel is His name. (Is. 47:4).

Their Redeemer is strong, the Lord of Hosts is His name. (Jer. 50:34).

Let the words of my mouth and the meditations of my heart, be acceptable before Thee, my Rock and my Redeemer. (Ps. 19:15).

And they remembered that God was their Rock, and the Most High, their Redeemer. (Ps. 78:35).

In the Christian tradition, Jesus Christ becomes the intermediary between man and God. Man can approach God only thru Jesus. Many years ago, a Christian friend of mine whose family was Jewish, passed away. I happened to be with him the day before he died and he requested me to ask his pastor to give a prayer at the funeral but not to mention the name of the "Savior" because he feared that it might be embarrassing to his family. I relayed the request to the minister of his church, and was surprised when he told me that he could not come to the funeral to give the prayer because of the condition imposed. "I cannot approach the Throne of Glory," he told me, "except thru Jesus Christ." Judaism teaches that every human being may and should approach God directly, without an intermediary.

Over and over again, the Jew is reminded that God alone is his savior, that "there is none like unto Him," and that a child of the Most High does not need an intermediary but can himself approach God, as Shepherd, Redeemer, Guardian and Father. The Bible abounds in passages like the following:

"Pardon, I pray Thee the iniquity of this people, according unto the greatness of Thy loving kindness, as Thou hast forgiven this people from Egypt until now. And the Lord said: 'I have pardoned'." (Nu. 14:19-20).

"And hearken Thou to the supplication of Thy servant, and of Thy people Israel, when they shall pray towards this place; yea, hear Thou in heaven Thy dwelling-place, and when Thou hearest, forgive." (I Kgs. 8:30).

"Seek ye the Lord, while He may be found,
Call upon Him while He is near;
Let the wicked forsake his way,
And the man of iniquity his thoughts.

48

And let him return unto the Lord, and He will have compassion upon him.

And to our God for He will abundantly pardon." (Is. 55:6-7).

"Return O Israel, unto the Lord Thy God,

For Thou has stumbled in Thine iniquity.

Take with you words

And return unto the Lord.

Say unto Him: 'Forgive all iniquity and accept that which is good,

For in Thee the fatherless findeth mercy!'

I will heal their backsliding

I will love them freely;

For Mine anger is turned away from him." (Hos. 14:2-5).

"Give ear, O Shepherd of Israel,

Thou that leadest Joseph like a flock,

And come and save us. O God restore us,

And cause Thy face to shine, and we shall be saved." (Ps. 80:2-4).

"As for me, I call upon Thee for Thou wilt answer me, O God.

Incline Thine ear unto me, hear my word.

As for me, I shall behold Thy face in righteousness.

I shall be satisfied when I awake, with Thy likeness." (Ps. 17:6, 15).

"Unto Thee, O God do I lift up my soul,

Show me Thy ways, O Lord,

Teach me Thy paths,

Guide me in Thy truth and teach me,

For Thou art the God of my salvation." (Ps. 25:4-5) .

Besides the Bible, the later literature—the Midrashic writings and the Talmud—contain innumerable statements that teach Jews to look to God alone as their redeemer and savior, stressing the Biblical passage: "The Lord God, merciful and gracious, long-suffering and abundant in goodness and ever true, keeping mercy for thousands, forgiving iniquity, transgression and sin." (Ex. 34:6-7) .

In the newly revised edition of the Union Prayer Book,[4] used in the Reform Jewish ritual, there is a beautiful prayer recited during the afternoon Service of Atonement Day. It contains a fine summary of the intimate relationship between a Jewish worshipper and his God. It runs thus: "O God, grant that we may hearken to the solemn admonition of this Sabbath of Sabbaths in true contrition of heart and humbleness of spirit. Help us to fulfill our obligation to the needy and the distressed. Incline our hearts to compassion, that we may aid the poor, the homeless and the suffering; help us to be as a father to the needy, eyes to the blind, and feet to the lame. Imbue us with an understanding of our responsibility to our brethren of the House of Israel and to the institutions which minister to their needs. Teach us to be generous in our support of all good works. Bless all who labor unselfishly for the welfare and happiness of their fellow men, and show Thy favor and Thy grace to all who serve Thee in truth and faithfulness. On this Day of Repentance, we return to Thee with chastened heart; receive us with favor, O God, our Father and our King, our Redeemer and our Savior, Amen."

VI.

The liberal Jew judges Bible events according to the scientific biblical standards of modern times. He has the same skeptical attitude towards the miraculous in the life and acts of Jesus, that he has towards the miracles of the Old Testament. Those that can be explained on a psychological, historical or rational basis, he accepts. The others he rejects. So with the miracles of the New Testament. His attitude towards the ascension of Jesus, is no different from that of his attitude towards the ascension of Elijah. His judgment concerning the miraculous cures of Jesus, is no different from that concerning the miracles performed by Elijah or by Elisha. When such a Jew considers the supernatural, he has the same questioning attitude towards the New Testament that he has towards the Old. Thus, of course, all supernatural elements involved in the stories of Jesus, are excluded. He is judged by the value of his teachings, which are assumed to be just as historical as are those of the teachers of the Old Testament. The authenticity of the documents and the historicity of the personalities need not trouble us in arriving at our value judgments. These need be based only on the texts that we have. We judge and evaluate what we have in our Bible just as we read and understand and believe other sources of knowledge and inspiration.

On the basis of Jesus's teachings as handed down, and of what we know of his life, a liberal Jew has a wholesome regard for the New Testament teacher. He knows that he was an enthusiastic, loyal and religious Jew, in whose heart burned an intense loyalty to Israel and Israel's faith.[1] He believes that this teacher, full of hope and with a vibrant love for his religion and his people, set out to do his chosen work with a consecrated heart, and traveled about recalling the (Mt. 10:6) "lost sheep of the house of Israel." A learned Jew knows that Jesus preached an idealistic and a prophetic-[2] Pharisaic[3] Judaism—in spite of some contested anti-Pharisaic passages in the New Testament. The words of Jesus (Mt. 5:17), "Think not that I am come to destroy the law, or the prophets; I am come not to destroy but to fulfill," surely do not indicate that Jesus had any idea of doing away with the commandments and the statutes and the teachings which were so dear to him and to the other Jews. The expression in the original Hebrew used by Jesus doubtless was "le-qa-yem ha-mitz-woth," means the "activating, the performing or the carrying out of the commandments."

The phrase does not mean "fulfill" in the sense of "completing" the commandments. It is frequently maintained by Christian scholars that the Law and the Prophets were not "complete," and the statement of Jesus means to say that he "completed or fulfilled," the Scriptures. Jesus had not the remotest reference to this thought. "Fulfilling the commandments" in the sense of "fulfilling or doing them," that is, doing what they demanded, was a universally used phrase, and Jesus repeated it, as was perfectly natural. Dr. Edgar Johnson Goodspeed has, in this case as he has in many others, caught more of the original meaning when he renders this passage in his translation of the New Testament, as follows: "I have not come to do away with them, but to enforce them." This, it seems to me, is somewhat nearer to the real thought in the mind of Jesus. When a Jew used the words "le-qa-yem ha-mitz-woth" he meant to say that he was to execute, that is, to carry out the intent of the commandments. It is certain in my mind, that Jesus did not intend to convey the idea that the commandments in the Torah—the Law—were incomplete or inadequate, and that he came to finish or to perfect them. To do the "mitzwos," to fulfill the commandments, is even now a common expression among pious Jews. The Gospel editors were unacquainted with this Hebrew expression and its meaning. Another similar outstanding error on the part of the translator or editor is the use of the word "lawyer" (Mt. 22:35; Lk. 10:25), "Then one of them who was a lawyer, asked," etc. The questioner was not a "lawyer"; he was a "ben Torah," a son of the Law, that is, a student of the Law, or as was meant, a "scholar." Even today, a man who is well-versed in Jewish tradition, is called a "ben Torah, a scholar." In many cases the real meaning of the words of Jesus, can be understood only if translated back into the original Hebrew or Aramaic.

And he sought to teach his listeners how to "fulfill the commandments." He was evidently an inspiring teacher. He was a lover of men and he drew to himself many of those whom others avoided. We have no records of other Jewish teachers fraternizing with publicans and sinners. The prophets did most eloquently preach justice and love. The Psalmists have tender passages concerning the poor and the meek.

Moses did not forget love for God and man, even the daily hire of the workman, nor kindness even to dumb animals. But Jesus was the first, I believe, actually to form friendships with those who by their unconventional life had drawn upon themselves the contempt and scorn of the pious and the strict. He was the first of the Jewish teachers to activate individually a teaching which later became universal, viz: "although he has sinned, he is still an Israelite." Jesus preached to those who would listen, while the rabbis taught those rather who answered the call of piety, scholarship and position. The outstanding original contribution of Jesus was his humane attitude towards those whom the rabbis and other teachers are accustomed to avoid or condemn. He felt it his duty to bring his message to the poor and the rejected, because, like the gentle Hillel, he loved all the children of the Father. He wanted to win to God all whom he addressed, and thus he pleaded for preparation for the Kingdom which he expected might come at any time. "Therefore be ye also ready; for in such an hour as you think not, the son of man cometh." (Mt. 24:44). Paul no doubt based upon the content of this verse, his own statement "that the day of the Lord so cometh as a thief in the night." (I Thes. 5:2).

Before this day was to come, Jesus gave himself up to the preaching of the "good tidings" of salvation, which was to be acquired by repentance and good deeds. It is quite evident that he did not consider deeply enough the difficulty into which he and his followers might come, insofar as the suspicion of the Romans was concerned. He did not realize what official Jewry well knew, that every Jewish leader who

could attract to himself a following was being watched by
the government, and to that extent he was a danger to all
of Israel. Jesus must have known that a number of Jewish
patriotic military leaders preceded him, and that they had
in one way or another been liquidated by the Romans. But
there can be no doubt that he felt that he was emphasizing
not this material world in which the Roman Government
was interested, but the spiritual world, the Kingdom of God.
And therefore, he regarded himself as safe from the penalty
that he must have known was meted out to those who could
be accused of preaching rebellion against Rome. For him,
the important thing, the Kingdom of Heaven, was at hand;
in fact, it had already begun. For "when he was demanded
of the Pharisees when the Kingdom of God cometh, he
answered them and said, 'the Kingdom of God cometh not
with observation; neither shall they say, 'lo here, or lo there';
for behold, the Kingdom of God is within you." (Lk. 17:20-
21). That is to say, the Kingdom of God was already on earth
in the hearts of those who repented and did good deeds.

And thus he went about calling upon his people to make
themselves ready for and worthy of the Kingdom predicted
by the prophets and apocalyptists, and expected almost any
hour. He had no thought for the things of the material world.
When a rich young man asked him what he should do to
inherit eternal life, Jesus told him to keep the commandments. When the inquirer answered that he had been doing
this from his youth, Jesus said, "one thing thou lackest; go,
sell whatever thou hast, and give to the poor, and thou shalt

have treasure in heaven, and come, take up the cross and follow me." (Mk. 10:21). There is no question in my mind that the word "cross" in this verse is not the word Jesus used. A "cross" would have had no meaning at all for Jesus—it was not a Jewish symbol. Jesus no doubt used a word that meant "burden" or "yoke." It was the later Christian writer or editor who used the word "cross." Jesus might have said "take upon yourself the yoke of the Torah" or "the yoke of the Kingdom of Heaven," both often used in Jewish tradition. To observe the personal commandments only and not to carry out what he regarded as also the essential will of God in humanizing society, was not enough. "Woe unto you who are rich, for you have received your consolation." (Lk. 6:24); and again, "Verily, I say unto you, it is easier for a camel to go thru a needle's eye, than for a rich man to enter into the Kingdom of God." (Mt. 19:23-24). The Gospels of Matthew and Luke do not have the words "come, take up the cross, and follow me," at all!

It is not difficult to understand why, according to the Gospels, Jesus had so strong a hold on the poor and the down-trodden. To have enough strength of purpose to drive away the rich who came to him, whose wealth he could so well have used for the daily needs of himself and his followers, because he believed that the rich would not inherit the world to come, is itself an act that would win the poor. And it must have been this very dedication to the social and spiritual message that he gave, that attracted to him all the "common people who gladly heard him." But dedication alone to a cause is not enough to have made the "multitude welcome him." There must have been a sincerity and a tenderness about him that evoked a great loyalty to him from his followers. His love for children, reminiscent of the statement in the prophecy of Isaiah, "and a little child shall lead them" (Is. 11:6), illustrated in several places, must also have impressed his disciples with his gentleness.

VII.

A Jew who is familiar with Jewish literature and the Gospels, knows that Jesus was the child of his Jewish training. One recalls the statement of Wellhausen, the great German Protestant Bible critic, quoted in Klausner's[1] "Jesus of Nazareth": "Jesus was not a Christian; he was a Jew. He did not preach a new faith, but taught men to do the will of God; and in his opinion and also in that of the Jews, the will of God was to be found in the Law of Moses and the other books of the Scripture." One of the greatest of American Christian New Testament scholars, the late Shirley Jackson Case,[2] wrote extensively to show that Jesus was the child of his day, that is to say, the child of Jewish teachers and Jewish training. His Jewishness has never been doubted by eminent students of his life, nor have most of his teachings, when compared with the Judaism of his contemporaries. It was only later that he was separated from his own, by the Christians of Gentile origin who were unfamiliar with his life and with the Jewish teachings which he quoted often, and of which he must have had a good general knowledge. It has already been noted that his followers never regarded him as anything but a loyal and professing Jew during his lifetime, though he differed in their interpretations with some of the Pharisees and with the Sadducees, as did many other teachers.

The most important evidence of the fact that Jesus never thought of himself as anything but a Jew, and that he never wanted to depart from the tradition of Moses and the Prophets, is the passage of which a part has already been cited in the Sermon on the Mount: "Think not that I came to destroy the Law or the Prophets. I came not to destroy but to fulfill. For verily I say unto you till heaven and earth pass away, one jot or one tittle shall in no wise pass away from the Law (the Torah), till all things be accomplished. Whosoever, therefore, shall break one of the least commandments, and shall teach men so, shall be called least in the Kingdom of Heaven." (Mt. 5:17-19). There are instances when Jesus and the disciples did not observe some of the customs or ceremonials that the Pharisees cherished, but that was not an uncommon thing. The Pharisees themselves did not agree on all matters. The disputes in the Mishnaic and Talmudic literature bear ample testimony to this. To assume, therefore, that Jesus was un-Jewish because, for instance, he permitted his disciples to pluck corn on the Sabbath, or because he healed people on the Sabbath, or because he ate with unwashed hands, or associated with these sinners who might have broken some commandments, is unwarranted.

This certainly does not justify the assumption that Jesus forsook his people and his religion and established a new one! Modern liberal Jewry agrees with Jesus in his attitude towards a superfluity of ceremonial detail. Reform Judaism has done away with much of that kind of minutiae which became a burden and has no ethical or spiritual value today. It cannot be too often emphasized that the tradition which has become so prevalent, that Jesus was the first Christian, is completely unhistorical. Jesus, as the central personality in the beginnings of Christianity, was the least conscious of all, that he might be the central figure in a new religion. He certainly never dreamt that this religion would be hostile to that into which he was born, by which he lived, and in which he died, and to his brethren who confessed it!

Modern informed Jews, accept most of the ethical teachings of Jesus. However, there are some which they do not accept—neither does most of the Christian world. For example, the principle of non-resistance, in the verses, "Ye have heard that it was said, 'an eye for an eye and a tooth for a tooth'; but I say unto you resist not him that is evil; but whosoever smiteth thee on thy right cheek, turn to him the other also, and if any man sue thee at law and take away thy coat, let him have thy cloak also. And whoever shall compel thee to go one mile, go with him twain." (Mt. 5:38-41). This principle of non-resistance is almost impossible in the kind of a world in which humans like us live. The Jew does not often comply with this teaching, and certainly Christians have paid little attention to it. Here and there, a few devoted souls, like the Essenes of Jesus' day and Ghandi and Albert Schweitzer of our own, have tried to live a non-resistant life. History does not attest to any great success.

59

Nor does the average man of today accept the idea of "good for evil," as enunciated in the same chapter, and in its parallel, the sixth of Luke. Matthew has it thus (5:43) : "Ye have heard that it was said, 'thou shalt love thy neighbor, and hate thine enemy.' But I say unto you, love your enemies, and pray for them that persecute you; that you may be sons of your Father which is in heaven." The quotation which Jesus cites here as having been "heard," presumably from the Jewish Scriptures, has never been found anywhere in Jewish literature, and scholars are unable to find even a trace of it. The passage in Luke which is parallel to this one (6:27-35) does not cite this verse, but substitutes the Golden Rule which is found in the seventh chapter of Matthew.

This teaching, too, has been largely ignored by the followers of Jesus as well as by Jews. There is a theory that the "good for evil" principle of Jesus was an adaptation from an old rabbinical statement, that one should act "lifnim meshurat haddin," meaning "beyond the limitations of justice," that is to say, act more than justly in any given circumstance.

Returning good for evil generally and universally is as little probable for human society as is non-resistance to evil. The Golden Rule of Hillel,[3] "What is hateful unto thee do not do unto thy neighbor" is equally idealistic. Hillel lived from about 50 B.C.E. to 10 of the common era. It is quite possible, and many scholars think probable, that Jesus may not only have known this liberal and beloved teacher, but may have been one of his students. Regarding the passage, "ye have heard that it was said," etc. (Mt. 5:43), there are verses in the Old Testament which point out the virtue of returning good for evil. One recalls these in the Book of Exodus: "If thou meet thine enemy's ox or ass going astray, thou shalt surely bring it back to him." (23:4-5). "If thou seest the ass of him that hateth thee lying under his burden, and wouldst forbear to help him, thou shalt surely help with him." In the Book of Proverbs we find several passages: "Say not, 'I will requite evil'; wait for the Lord. He will save thee" (20:22); "Rejoice not when thine enemy falleth; and let not thine heart be glad when he stumbleth; lest the Lord see it, and it displease Him" (24:17-18); "Say not: 'I will do so to him as he hath done unto me; I will render to the man according to his work'" (24:29); "If thine enemy be hungry, give him bread to eat, and if he be thirsty give him water to drink; for thou wilt heap coals of fire upon his head, and the Lord will reward thee" (25:21).

We do not agree wholly with Jesus in his attitude towards Gentiles when he charges his disciples "not to go into any way of the Gentiles, and not to enter any city of the Samaritans, but rather to go to the lost sheep of the House of Israel. And as ye go, preach, saying, 'the Kingdom of Heaven is at hand. Heal the sick, raise the dead, cleanse the lepers, cast out devils; freely ye received, freely give'." (Mt. 10:5-8). These services he intended only, according to this passage, for fellow-Jews. In his journey towards Tyre and Sidon, we read: "A Gentile, a Syro-Phoenician by race, whose little daughter had an unclean spirit besought him that he should cast forth the demon out of her daughter. And he said to her, 'let the children first be filled; for it is not meet to take the children's bread and cast it to the dogs.' But she answered and saith unto him, 'Yea, Lord, even the dogs under the table eat of the children's crumbs.' And he said unto her, 'for this saying, go thy way; the devil is gone out of thy daughter.' And she went away unto her house and found the child laid upon the bed and the devil gone out." (Mk. 7:24-30). Surely Jesus did not mean to call the Gentile children "dogs" which must be fed only after Jewish children were sated! It would be a harsh and unfriendly thing to say. But as a matter of gospel-history, however, Jesus was primarily concerned about Jews and healed only a few non-Jewish persons. One was the child of the Syro-Phoenician, and another was a servant of the centurion of Capernaum (Mt. 9:13).

It seems difficult for a Christian to understand that Jesus was at all times a most faithful Jew who was concerned to the utmost about his own people and their spiritual life first. He was not particularly interested in Gentiles and in the world at large. He was not concerned with Rome except insofar as it was a cruel master of Judea. He yearned for an Israel that would repent of its sins, pray with sincerity, execute the commandments, and thus bring about that kingdom which was already in the hearts of those who devoted themselves to prayer and to the practices enjoined by the Law and the Prophets.

A Jew of today, like his ancestor in the ancient times and like most people in our day, would not concur with Jesus in the economic messianism which he preached. The teaching to get rid of what one owned (Mk. 10:21); the penalty that the rich man had to pay for being wealthy while the poor Lazarus went to the bosom of Abraham (Lk. 16:19-31); the emphasis in several places upon the bliss of the "poor" and those that "hunger," in contrast to the woes against the rich and the self-satisfied—these ideas were not accepted to any wide extent in his day, and neither are many Jews nor Christians guided by them today.

With the increased desire for universal peace, and with the constant peril of war before us, it is difficult to agree with the parallel statements describing the mission of Jesus in Matthew (10:34-38) and Luke (12:51-53) which we quote: "Think not that I came to send peace on earth; I came not to send peace, but a sword. For I came to set a man at variance against his father, and the daughter against her mother, and the daughter-in-law against her mother-in-law; and a man's foes shall be they of his own household." The terrible persecutions in the name of religion have highlighted these words, though probably Jesus never intended these horrible injustices. Liberal Jews and liberal Christians cannot accept these miscarriages of religion as the mission of the looked-for Messiah! Some Christian scholars believe that these words were not spoken by Jesus, and some explain them away as being in some way figurative. One however cannot expunge Bible passages one does not like, or make them fit particular individual theories or points of view. If this were done, chaos in Biblical criticism would result. Biblical interpretation, too, has its limitations.

The same attitude applies to Jesus' rejection of his mother

and his brethren as stated in all the Synoptic Gospels. We quote (Mt. 12:46-50): "While he was yet speaking to the multitudes, behold, his mother and his brethren stood without, seeking to speak to him. And one said to him, 'behold thy mother and thy brethren stand without, seeking to speak to thee.' But he answered and said unto him that told him: 'Who is my mother, and who are my brethren?' And he stretched forth his hands toward his disciples and said: 'Behold my mother and my brethren. For whosoever shall do the will of my Father which is in heaven, he is my brother, and sister and mother'." The inculcation for thousands of years of the basic importance of family life; countless centuries' emphasis on the kinship of the family and the relationship of father, mother and children as the basis of human society, make it difficult to understand an attitude which would permit the breaking up of the tender ties of family unity. Certainly there are some who have placed the love of a personal ideal above love for family and friends and have by so doing benefitted the world. Yet if there were a continuous breaking-up of family-ties even for the pursuit of an ideal, the foundation of human society would be destroyed. Such a course is permissible in isolated cases; but it means the destruction of the very basis of social life as we know it now, if it becomes a universal habit.

It is almost impossible to believe that Jesus would thus publicly have violated one of the most important commandments of the Decalogue, which has always been and still is one of the most prized possessions of Judaism. Next to a belief in God, a Jewish child was taught the Fifth Command-

ment which begins: "Honor thy father and thy mother."
(Ex. 20:12; Dt. 5:16).

VIII.

The ethics of Jesus in general stand out as a great light
in the path of civilization. His "first commandment" was
given in an answer, in (Mt. 22:34-38) to the Pharisees, and
in (Mk. 12:28-31), to a scribe. We quote from Mark: "And
one of the scribes came, and heard them questioning together, and knowing that he had answered them well, asked
him, 'what commandment is the first of all?' Jesus answered,
'The first is, 'Hear O Israel, the Lord our God, the Lord is
One; and thou shalt love the Lord thy God, with all thy
heart, and with all thy soul, with all thy mind and with all
thy strength'." This passage is almost an exact repetition of
the most fundamental of all prayers in the Jewish prayer
book. It is taken from Deuteronomy (6:4-5) and has held
its primacy in the many different Jewish prayer-books which
have been compiled. We do not know exactly when the
earliest prayer-book was completed; but from the earliest
extant prayer manuals until the latest edited in our own
day, this statement of the Unity of God, with the addition
of verses 6-9, have been universally and unquestionably repeated and regarded as of greatest importance. As long as
Judaism maintains its belief in One God and cherishes a
reverence for its Scriptures, these teachings will hold the

chief place in its articles of faith. The first teaching of
Judaism that a child learns, and the last thing that a dying
Jew, if conscious, recites, is this prayer, known as the
"Shema;" and it holds for us exactly the same degree of
importance now that it held for Jesus—the first place in the
Jewish credo, the first "commandment."

The commandment which Jesus points out as the second
in importance, is "Thou shalt love thy neighbor as thyself."
(Lev. 19:18). Both Matthew (22:39-40) and Mark (12:31)
mention this commandment. The thought in the verses in
Matthew, namely, "And a second like unto it, is this: 'Thou
shalt love thy neighbor as thyself,' on these two commandments hangeth the whole law and the prophets," approaches
very closely the answer of Hillel, who when asked by a
heathen to teach him Judaism while he stands on one foot
said:[1] "What is hateful unto thee, do not do unto thy neighbor. That is the whole law. All else is commentary; go and
learn." And in another place we have it that Rabbi Akiba
taught,[2] "Thou shalt love thy neighbor as thyself; this is
the greatest commandment in the Torah." Judaism here,
ancient and modern, stands with Jesus. Unfortunately,
neither Jews nor Christians nor others, have in reality prac-
ticed the teaching expressed in it.

A liberal Jew of today certainly is in accord with the ideal
of Jesus as expressed in the phrases, Kingdom of Heaven or
Kingdom of God. This concept, phrased also in the Hebrew
as the Kingdom of Heaven, has been the hope of the House
of Israel ever since prophetic times. The Messiah was to reign
over the earth, which was to be a place of justice, righteous-

ness and peace, in which the "knowledge of God would fill the earth as the waters cover the sea." (Is. 11:9). In the days of the expectation of the Messiah, the kingdom was to be of this world. The land of Israel was to be ruled, as noted, by a scion of the House of David, a righteous king such as is described by the prophet Isaiah and others. This Messiah, called the King-Messiah, was to activate the commandments of the Torah and the Prophets, and to make Israel the great example of the perfect state, to all the nations. Jesus like his contemporaries, believed what the Lord said thru Isaiah (1:24-27, 2:3) and yearned for its consummation: "I will ease Me of Mine adversaries and avenge Me of Mine enemies; and I will turn My hand upon thee, and purge away thy dross as with lye, and will take away all thine alloy. And I will restore thy judges as at first, and thy counselors as at the beginning. Afterward thou shalt be called the city of righteousness, the faithful city; Zion shall be redeemed with justice, and they that repent, with righteousness . . . for out of Zion shall go forth the Law, and the word of the Lord, from Jerusalem."

The evil days in which Jesus lived and which preceded and followed him, came upon Israel, our ancestors believed, because it had departed[3] from the commandments of God (Dt. XXVIII, and prophetic passages). Jesus was certain of this, as were the Pharisees. Salvation would come only after repentance and a return to God. The time of the coming of the Kingdom was in the hands of God, and the certainty of its coming was in the minds of the people. If the house of

Israel would give up its unrighteous living, its sinful conduct, its uncharitableness, its selfishness and desire for wealth; if it truly worshipped God, treated its widows and orphans and poor with justice; if it returned to God as in the days of yore, the Day of Judgment would come and the messianic period would be ushered in, and the Kingdom of God, under the King-Messiah, would be established. This was the vision of Jesus as well as that of his contemporaries.

In its main outlines we can agree with the Kingdom idea. The era of peace and brotherliness is the very heart of traditional and modern Judaism, as it is the goal of the ethical teachings of Jesus. Jews today differ in some details in their conception of the Kingdom from that of their Jewish forebears and from that of Jesus. Details are unimportant. Reform Judaism has substituted for the concept of the personal Messiah, the idea of the "messianic era," to denote that it no longer shares the belief in a personal Messiah, and teaches that each one of us can help to bring about the "messianic era," by living the kind of life that will bring us the Kingdom of Heaven. Jesus himself was not consistent at all times, according to the statements ascribed to him by the Gospels, in his conception of the Kingdom. As a matter of fact, while he was insistent upon its coming, he had never given a detailed amplification of what he really meant. The reason probably was that there was a generally accepted meaning of the concept, and it needed no explanation. All except some Sadducees believed that the terrible plight caused by Roman rule was at last to give way to a reign of peace and happiness—the kingdom of righteousness, justice, loving-kindness, and holiness; and this reign was to be brought about by repentance, good deeds and prayer. Differences in the general messianic conception centered about the person of the Messiah, not about his coming and his role.

One of the most famous and inspiring passages of the New Testament, is the Lord's Prayer. The more popular version is (Mt. 6-9:15) : "Our Father which art in Heaven, hallowed be thy Name, Thy kingdom come, Thy will be done on earth as it is in heaven. Give us this day our daily bread, and forgive us our debts, as we forgive our debtors. And lead us not into temptation, but deliver us from evil, for Thine is the Kingdom and the power and the glory forever, Amen." The prayer in Luke (11:2-4) is shorter, and stops with "evil." The Prayer is in every way Jewish. Its contents have been borrowed from Jewish pre-Christian sources. Grotius, a great seventeenth century Christian scholar, expressed the view that the Prayer "was a combination of Jewish prayers." In his excellent book, "Sources of the Sermon on the Mount," Gerald Friedlander says (Ch. X) : "the Encyclopedia Biblica states, 'the truth is, that we may say of the Lord's Prayer, applying what Theodore Zahn lately wrote of the teachings of Jesus as a whole, namely, that Jesus uttered things which were said almost literally by Jewish teachers before and after him'." Zahn was not a Jew. Claude Montefiore wrote that "whoever put it together chose with fine religious feeling and insight." There is not a single idea or expression which cannot be found in pre-Christian Jewish literature. The grouping of the expressions and even their choice may be original—and even that is doubted—but the meaning and essence are distinctively Jewish. There were other teachers who gave individual prayers. Their content was also, of course, Jewish, and that is, it seems to me, what really counts. But few compare to the Lord's Prayer in brevity, grandeur, directness and intimate appeal.

One can only say that the main reason for Jews not reciting the Prayer is that it has become so intimately connected with Christian usage, that the Synagog will not accept it as part of its ritual. There is no other reason for not reclaiming that which is thoroughly and theologically Jewish. Many liberal Jews feel no hesitancy in joining their Christian brethren on occasions when the Prayer is recited in unison.

There are many other teachings of Jesus with which Jews agree and which they hail as powerful instruments in giving man a higher conception of religion. Such are his emphasis on truth; on alms-giving for the good it does, rather than for exhibition purposes; on sincerity in prayer and fasting, unmixed with hypocrisy; on care and justice in pronouncing judgment upon others; on the Golden Rule principle; on the teaching that "not what goes into the mouth defiles a man, but that which comes out of the mouth—evil thoughts, murders, adulteries, fornications, thefts, false witness, blasphemies; these are the things that defile man." (Mt. 15:18-20; Mk. 7:18-23). We accept his emphasis on sacrifice in giving, as illustrated by the incident of the two coins given by the widow who was poor, and the lesson that he draws from this, namely, that this gift was more than that of the wealthy, because they had much more and therefore sacrificed less (Lk. 21:1-4) ; on the care men must exercise in accusing others of the fault which they themselves possess, as shown by the "beam" illustration (Mt. 7:3); on his insistence that we take care lest we condemn ourselves, as shown by the example of the woman taken in adultery, with his suggestion that he among the accusers who is without sin, be the first one to cast the stone in the stoning of the woman accused (Jn. 8:7). His attitude towards forgiveness—one must "forgive even if it is seventy times seven"—is magnificent beyond words (Mt. 18:22).

IX.

It is because time has brought healing to many of the wounds inflicted on Israel in the name of the Christian Christ, and because Christians themselves, including many high churchmen in both Catholic and Protestant Christianity have realized the great injustice that has been done to the kin of Jesus, that liberals on both sides of the great wall that has separated Jew and Christian, may now meet each other upon the basis of the appreciation of Jesus. None can deny the world-wide influence that his name has carried, and the change that his teachings have wrought. And there have been times long before our day, in which great Jewish thinkers have recognized and appreciated his teachings. The eminent philosopher, Moses Maimonides (1135-1204) was not afraid to say that it was the will of Divine Providence, that through Jesus and Christianity, the name of God was spread over the world. Other outstanding Jews have placed him among the world's greatest teachers. Some have even put him in the prophetic succession. Here are a few of the opinions expressed:

The most eminent of all Jewish historians, the German Dr. Heinrich Graetz, in his "History of the Jews," published in English translation, has this to say, among other things, of Jesus: "Jesus made no attack upon Judaism itself, he had no idea of becoming the Reformer of Jewish doctrine or the propounder of a new law; he sought merely to redeem the sinner, to call him to a good and holy life, to teach him that he is a child of God, and to prepare him for the approaching messianic time. He insisted upon the unity of God, and was far from attempting to change in the slightest degree the Jewish conception of the Deity. The merit of Jesus consists especially in his efforts to impart greater inner force to the precepts of Judaism, in the enthusiasm with which he obeyed them himself, in his ardor to make the Judeans turn to God with filial love as children to their father, in his fervent upholding of the brotherhood of man, in his insistence that moral laws be placed in the foreground, and in his endeavors to have them accepted by those who had been hitherto regarded as the lowest and most degraded of human beings." (Vol. II:155-156).

Claude G. Montefiore, an outstanding English Jewish scholar and Bible commentator, who wrote a three volume commentary on the Gospels (The Synoptic Gospels, London, 1909), says this (Vol. II, p. 1098): "Yet the time will surely come when the role of Israel's prophets will be acknowledged by Jews themselves not to close before the Prophet of Nazareth. Not Malachi, but Jesus will be spoken of as 'the last of the prophets.' For here is his true spiritual kinship; he is of the same stuff and lineage as Amos, Hosea and Isaiah. . . . Modern Judaism needs both the rabbis and Jesus. It can, as it were, absorb both of them. Both are bone of the Jewish bone, and spirit of the Jewish spirit." I would not go as far as Montefiore and make so general a statement. I should not classify Jesus among the Major Prophets. But I would unhesitatingly include him with some of the Minor Prophets.

In our country, there have been many influential Jewish voices who have maintained a friendly attitude towards the man of Nazareth. Some of its most eminent rabbis and teachers have expressed a truly liberal attitude towards him. Dr. K. Kohler, for many years president of the Hebrew Union College where the Reform Rabbis of the country are trained, wrote in his epoch-making book, "Jewish Theology" (New York, 1918, p. 434): "The young Nazarene manifested as preacher and healer of the sick, a profound love for, and tender sympathy with suffering humanity, a trait fostered among the Essenes. . . . His simple countrymen, the fishers and shepherds of Galilee, on hearing his wise and humane teachings and seeing his miraculous cures, considered him a prophet and conqueror of the host of demons, the workers of disease. In contrast to the learned Pharisees, he felt it to be his calling to bring the good tidings of salvation to the poor and the outcast to 'seek the lost sheep of the house of Israel' and win them for God."

In the book entitled "My Religion" (N. Y. 1925, p. 64),
the late Rabbi Emil G. Hirsch states: "The poets who created Jesus intended to make him the greatest and most
typical Jew, and he was the greatest and most typical Jew,
if he ever lived. . . ." He then quotes his father, Dr. Samuel
Hirsch, a great German-American theologian, as follows: "In
Jesus we have the creation of a character molded exactly
according to the pattern of Judaism; in Jesus, we have the
typical, the ideal Jew; we have no reason for rejecting him
as a teacher or even exemplar, and yet we must not forget
that the ideal Jew pictured in the Gospels has his limitations,
limitations due to time and circumstance." Dr. Emil G.
Hirsch then observes that "in that light, we must study this
poetic, this artistic so-called biography of the master of
Nazareth. We Jews never rejected him, we have no cause to
reject him. He was a Jew if ever there was a Jew, a loyal
Jew in every respect, and his life was thoroughly Jewish."

Dr. Hyman Enelow said in his volume, "A Jewish View
of Jesus" (N. Y. 1931, p. 177): "Touching the Judaism of
Jesus, one must bear this in mind. It does not mean that
Jesus was any less in harmony with Judaism because he
accentuated in his teachings the elements of love, of kindness,
of brotherliness, of indifference to the material world with
its cares and rewards. He thus taught a phase of religion that
was part of Judaism, and that has formed the most precious
part of it to many a Jewish devotee. The modern Jew, therefore, cannot fail to appreciate Jesus as a religious and ethical
teacher."

In 1919 the author of this book published his "Judaism,

Christianity and the Modern Social Ideals." He wrote (p. 264): "The liberal Jew of today regards Jesus not as the Messiah, not as the Son of God and the Redeemer of mankind, and not as the perfect or Ideal Man. But he looks upon him as a Jewish teacher of the first century, human in his passions, devoted to his religion, enthusiastic for its advancement, loyal to its implications and sincere in his admiration for it. For all of these, the liberal Jew admires Jesus; further he cannot go. He cannot give him a place beside the Creator of the Universe and call him 'Lord.' For to the Jew, 'God will always be One and His Name will be One'." (Zech. 14:9).

In a remarkable work, "Jesus of Nazareth, His Life, Times and Teachings," Dr. Joseph Klausner, formerly of the Hebrew University of Jerusalem, says: "In his ethical code there is a sublimity, distinctiveness and originality in form unparalleled in any other Hebrew ethical code; neither is there any parallel to the remarkable art of his parables. The shrewdness and sharpness of his proverbs and his forceful epigrams serve in exceptional degree, to make ethical ideas a popular possession. If ever the day should come and this ethical code be stripped of its wrappings of miracles and mysticism, the Book of the Ethics of Jesus will be one of the choicest treasures in the literature of Israel for all time." This is one of the greatest of all tributes to Jesus, because Dr. Klausner is a great, as well as devout, Orthodox Jew, who dedicated his whole life to Jewish learning and who, in the days when it was not popular for Jews to write about Jesus, and in Jerusalem at that, wrote his famous volume.

I regard Klausner's work as the most authentic and scholarly of all the lives of Jesus.

X.

I have discussed with innumerable Jewish friends, their attitude towards the man of Nazareth. There is a very evident feeling on their part that he has been greatly misunderstood by those who call themselves his followers. I find that there is a much better feeling towards him than there is towards the prophets on the part of Christians. They share with Christians the truth of his desire and mission to make this a better world through the coming of the Kingdom. In this respect Christians have not, to a very large extent, been his real disciples. But for this the Man of Nazareth is not to blame. Singularly, the real disciples of Jesus have been his own flesh and blood who have borne the whips and lashes of torture and persecution, and yet, like their great kinsman, have not given up faith either in God or in the Kingdom.

The attitude of liberal Jews has been fostered not only by the opinions of outstanding liberal leaders of the Jewish faith, but by two of the greatest personalities of Orthodox Judaism. One as noted, is Prof. Klausner, and the other is the great literary light, Sholom Asch. Asch as well as Klausner, have gone to the original sources and have given the world the benefit of their researches. The effect has been to educate people to the fact that Jesus is not to be blamed for the errors of his followers. It is well known now that it was later Gentile-Christian misinterpretations of the teachings of Jesus that were responsible for the blindness and malice that resulted in the deep-seated prejudice, the vicious malice and the murderous hatred against the Jewish people. Surely for these, the man of Nazareth could not be held responsible. It would have been difficult to convince the victims of persecution of this, because even as they were tortured, they were told that their punishment was inflicted in the name of Christ and Christianity for their "blindness."

For those non-Jews who feel the injustice of the false accusations and the religious views which have been held and which they would gladly see changed, it is not enough just to conclude that they were wrong, and stop there. There is another sacred duty. Children hear things that we do not suspect they hear, and they learn things that later often shock us. No child is born with prejudice—whether against national, racial or religious differences, whether against a colored or a Jewish or a foreign child. A child has somewhere heard—it did not invent—the word "Christ-killer," the accusation that Jews killed Christ. But it soon learns when to use it. When it catches the attitude of its parents, it accepts it until it learns to think for itself. The result of early conditioning and training is so strong that only by a great effort—which many do not care to exert—does it rid itself of early prejudices, heard and acquired. In the realm of proper children's education lies a sacred duty of the liberal Christians.

This study is presented with the hope that misunderstandings with regard to Jesus and his teachings may be cleared away and friendlier feelings created on the part of those who differ. We know, however, that religious beliefs are slow to change, especially among those whose religious thinking is determined by unchanging tradition, and who accept that tradition unquestioningly. Orthodox religions are conservative and suspicious of new and changing concepts which affect the faith of their devotees. It takes a long time for research and new discovery to break through the mass of accumulated beliefs.

It is not many centuries since many Christian children were taught to avoid Jews because they were the children of the devil. It is not long since some Jewish children were taught to avoid even passing a Christian church because it was the center of hatred of Jews. If in another day a Jew trembled when he passed a church, it was because the church reminded him of the time when his people were put to a ruthless sword often led by a cross-bearer, or suffered in Russian pogroms, led by a fanatic cleric. One of my own grandmothers testified to having gone thru one of these horrors.

There are still some parts of Europe where people believe that Jews use Christian blood for Passover. That libel involving Jews in America, was even circulated in our country a few years ago and queries were actually received by Jews as to the truth of the story. And how many people even now erroneously believe that the Jews, not the Romans, killed Jesus!

We believe that as time goes on, the Jews will include

Jesus among their great teachers, as indicated by Klausner and Montefiore. We believe that as western civilization progresses, Jews and Christians, getting a more historical knowledge of the real teachings of Jesus, will help to create a better and more peaceful world. When the truth is learned by the professors of both religions, it will prevail.

Long-held prejudices are not easily eradicated. It often takes almost a lifetime to free one's self of a personal misjudgment. How can we expect hatreds that have lasted centuries to be wiped out quickly from the consciousness of the masses? Peoples as well as individuals must undergo mentally therapeutic discipline to eradicate their false judgments, as must those who have suffered from them, if they want to forget and forgive. Religious prejudice is often more difficult to dissipate than any other, in spite of the fact that religion is supposed to teach tolerance and love.

There is much to be done towards achieving good-will towards each other in our land, particularly in the field of Jewish-Christian relations. The United States, which has set an example by aiding many nations materially, can do this also in our own spiritual sphere. Let us be courageous enough at least to try to eliminate the historical errors that have erected walls of ignorance and suspicion in the religious field. And among the most important of these unfriendly differences are the conflicting opinions about Jesus and his teachings, about beliefs of the Jews, and about their reasons for rejecting the Pauline doctrines. Progress along this line which will wipe out bigotry, cruelty and misunderstanding is inevitable in a world that believes in better human relationships—in a world that yearns as did its greatest teachers including Jesus, for the establishment of peace and the Kingdom of God.

II.

Why and By Whom Was Jesus Crucified

I.

ONE WHO IS interested in the life and teachings of Jesus, will naturally ask: "Why and by whom was Jesus crucified?" A correct historical answer is helpful to a more complete understanding of his life and teachings. The following pages will give us an unbiased account of the deliberate and vicious misinterpretation of the words of the teacher to justify a barbarous political murder of an innocent idealist.

It has been repeated innumerable times that Jesus was born, lived and died a Jew. There was never the slightest intimation, either by him or by his immediate disciples, that he was anything else. His dominating interest in his adult life was his religion, or if you will, his people, which in the end, means the same thing. Like millions of his coreligionists before and after him, he died, a sacrifice for his faith and for his kinsmen.

While there is a great deal of doubt as to whether or not he considered himself the Messiah at or near the beginning of his ministry, it is apparent that towards the end, he did regard himself as the expected One of his people. At Caesarea

81

Philippi he asked his disciples: "Who do men say I am?" And they answered: "John the Baptist. But some say 'Elias', and others 'one of the prophets'." Then Jesus asks: "But who do you say that I am?" And Peter answers, "Thou art the Christ."[1] The three synoptic Gospels, that is, Matthew, Mark and Luke, contain essentially the same account. But he charged his disciples not to tell anyone about this. In passages similar to that of the one in Matthew where Jesus tells his questioners that "hereafter shall ye see the son of man sitting at the right hand of power, and coming in the clouds of heaven" (Mt. 26:64; Mk. 14:62), Jesus definitely declares himself the Messiah, the son of God. In the Old Testament, the expression "son of man" usually means a human being, except in the Book of Daniel (Dan. 7:2), where there is some doubt as to the expression's exact meaning. In the Gospel of John which is the latest and considered the least historical of the Gospels, Jesus speaks of himself definitely as the "light of the world, as the one sent by God, and says that he was not of this world." (Jn. 8:12 and similar passages).

On the way from Jericho to Jerusalem, Bartimeus, a blind man, salutes Jesus as "thou son of David, have mercy on me."[2] Jesus healed him saying "Go thy way, thy faith hath made thee whole." The accounts in Matthew and Luke are somewhat different, but essentially they are similar. Jesus accepts the appellation "son of David," which in the minds of the Judeans of that day meant a descendant of David who will be king. As the Passover Festival approaches, Jesus makes his way to Jerusalem. He finds the city filled with holiday worshippers and visitors. He does not come as an unknown teacher. He remembered the prophesy he has read in the Book of the Prophet Zechariah (Zech. 9:9), that the Messiah would come riding into Jerusalem upon an ass. Jesus rides into the city upon an ass[3] and is loudly acclaimed, the crowds crying "hosanna to the son of David; blessed is he that cometh in the name of the Lord; hosanna in the highest," according to the Gospel of Matthew. According to Mark the multitudes cried: "Blessed is he that cometh in the name of the Lord; hosanna in the highest." There is an interesting passage in (Lk. 19:39-40) which tells that some of the Pharisees asked Jesus to rebuke his disciples. They were evidently afraid that the plaudits of Jesus' followers and his very prophet-like entry into the city would arouse the Romans. They knew the mind of the enemy. The Sadduceans also watched the career of Jesus as it developed from the teacher and "prophet of Nazareth" to that of the "son of David."

There was no question now but that Jesus regarded himself as the Messiah—as did his disciples. He began to act out this role. He predicted that the messianic time was imminent and that the city would be destroyed. He entered the Temple and "cleansed" it. He assumed authority as if being directly sent by God. He even violated some of the traditional usages and customs because he felt that he was the "Son of the Father." This was Passover time. It was Israel's festival of freedom—recalling the days that Moses the Teacher liberated the ancestors of these people from the yoke of the Egyptians. Had not many of Jesus' followers heard him tell in what is commonly designated as the "transfiguration," that a voice out of the clouds said[4] "this is my beloved son in whom I am well pleased, hear ye him"; and did he not charge them "tell the vision to no one, until the son of man be risen from the dead"? They had been told that "the son[5] of man hath power on earth to forgive sins." To one sick with palsey, he said: "Son, thy sins be forgiven." The forgiving of sins was the privilege of God alone—and in assuming this privilege Jesus acknowledged the implication that he was the "son of God." The Gospel of John has a curious statement implying divine power (Jn. 10:18): "No man taketh it (my life) from me, but I lay it down of myself. I have power to lay it down, and I have power to take it again. This commandment have I received from my Father." He had told his disciples that "there be some standing here which shall not taste of death, till they see the son of man coming in his kingdom."[6] And he pointed out that "whosoever shall be ashamed of me and of my words in this adulterous and sinful generation, the son of man also shall be ashamed of him, when he cometh in the glory of his Father with the angels." (Mk. 8:38; Lk. 9:26).

In his earlier ministry when Jesus had not yet made up his mind definitely that he was the Messiah, he cautioned his listeners and disciples not to spread the information that he was the "Christ." Now he definitely assumed the role. His instruction at Philippi, namely: "Then charged he the disciples that they should tell no man that he was Christ" (Mt. 16:20; Mk. 8:30; Lk. 9:21), was now a thing of the past.[7] The die had been cast. He was now openly and enthusiastically greeted by those who followed him as the one predicted in the literature and in the traditions which they accepted, and who were looking for the immediate appearance of the Messiah.

If the accounts in the Gospels were true, the entrance of Jesus into Jerusalem was not accidental, but a carefully thought-out plan. It was, as noted, at the time of the universally observed Festival of Freedom, the Passover when the city was filled with holiday pilgrims. He had been proclaimed by his followers as King-Messiah, the descendant of David, and to this he had raised no objection. He had come into the city in the manner in which tradition had pictured the entry of the Messiah—upon an ass, and he had willingly received messianic acclaim from his loyal followers. Many of the Pharisees in Jerusalem and in places where Jesus had been, knew this. It is nonsense to believe that the Pharisees as a whole, knew him or cared about his teachings. The Jerusalem Sadduceans, ever-watchful of events that might excite the Romans, knew about him. There was no doubt in the minds of the Jewish priestly Roman minions that the Roman authorities were aware of the activities of Jesus and his followers. In addition to the demonstrations of the disciples, came the "cleansing" of the Temple by Jesus. While the stories in the Gospels regarding this act do not appear to make it one of primary importance, as a matter of fact, in the eyes of the Sadducees and their Roman officials, it was. But an explanation is necessary to clarify the significance of this episode.

Besides the Holy of Holies in the Temple proper, there were also inner courts into which only the servants of the

Temple—that is, priests and Levites could enter. Then there were outer courts, chambers and stalls, which were accessible to all Jews. The general population milled about the outer Temple precincts where stalls containing the animals for the offerings were erected. This facility was particularly important around the time of the Pilgrim Festivals,[8] when there were many pilgrims in the city, who came to offer sacrifices, and for whom the necessary accommodations both for the purchase of animals and for the exchange of foreign monies had to be provided. But as a matter of fact, the traffic in animals and the exchange of monies were not permitted in the Temple proper, or in its inner courts. It is possible that some Sadducean priests who may have profited from the sale of animals or the renting of stalls, may have been lenient about permitting the erection of stalls or booths where they should not be. At any rate, there was apparently some haggling and money-changing which offended the sensibilities of Jesus, and he took matters into his own hands, and cleaned out the money-changers (Mt. 21:12-17; Mk. 11:15-19; Lk. 19:45-48).

This act on his part enraged the money-changers—and there must have been a large number of them—who had both a religious and a legal right to carry on their business in the stalls outside of the Temple proper, but within the Temple precincts. It angered Sadducean priests who saw here an illegal and impious desecration of the whole custom of ritualistic sacrifices and offerings which was the chief reason for the presence of the pilgrims at the festival. The Romans saw in this act a challenge of their authority, for the

Sadducean servants of the Temple were their favorites. Prof. Klausner observes:[9] "So orthodox a Christian scholar as Dalman is forced to admit that there is nowhere any mention that the priests trafficked with sacrificial animals. It was forbidden to bring money even within the Temple Mount. . . . The Romans allowed only small copper coins to be minted in Palestine, and the silver and gold coins of the time were stamped with the figure of the Emperor, making their use impossible in the Temple; and Jewish pilgrims from foreign parts brought all manner of coinage. For these two reasons money-changers were necessary near the Temple. Even to this day Jews sell the privilege of reading the blessings before and after the reading of the Law and Prophets, and Christians sell candles in their churches." He could have added that besides candles, many other religious objects are sold within the precincts of houses of worship; and in some, even games of chance are permitted in order to swell the ecclesiastical treasuries! But no one in our days has had the courage of Jesus to raid these churches, throw out those who permit this, and "overthrow the tables . . . and the seats" (Mt. 21:12; Mk. 11:15).

The gospel writers either because of their ignorance of the Temple area, or in order to enhance the courage of Jesus in the attack on the money-changers unfortunately make no distinction between the "holy" portions of the Temple and the outer courts. That is why those who read the stories of the "cleansing" think that the Temple attendants sanctioned trading in it. According to the tradition of the Pharisees, the booths for the sale of pigeons and doves were not in the Temple proper at all, but on the Hill of Anointing, that is, the Mount of Olives. I mention this because I have heard derisive remarks about the Temple in Jerusalem having become a market-place for loose trading and a den of thieves by animal "racketeers." This is not so. The Temple remained until its destruction, the depository of the Divine Presence, the holiest structure of the Jewish people. The interesting story of its cleansing by Jesus is the embellishment of the Gospel writers. Jesus no doubt did clean out some dishonest trading in the Temple precincts, but this is different from the Gospel story that the "Bet Hamikdash," the holy sanctuary, had become a "den of thieves."

II.

Jesus had angered some of the Pharisees in his arguments with them, but they could not punish him severely because in Pharisaism there was room for difference of opinion as is attested by the many different opinions expressed by the various rabbis in the Talmud. Contemporary and later rabbis disagreed vehemently in any number of interpretations, but there were no drastic penalties except in a few cases— never the death penalty for such disagreement. But Jesus' assumption of the role of Messiah-King, topped by his assault on the money-changers and the sacrificial-animal stalls, and by his enthusiastic following, combined to form a very serious crisis which frightened the Sadducean priests. It was nothing out of the ordinary to see Jews who assumed messianic pretensions and wanted to save their people, killed by sword or crucified. There was no dearth of contemporary patriots who started incipient riots, and some paid for them with their lives. Rome was ever watchful. It was for events like this that the Roman governors moved their court from Caesarea Philippi to Jerusalem at Passover time, and Pilate was no exception to the pattern carried out by his predecessors.

Jesus knew that he was being watched. He was familiar with Jewish history, and he was well aware of what would happen to him if he were accused and found guilty of treason to Rome. Pilate was not bothered about the controversies between Jesus and Pharisees. Priestly services and Temple sacrifices, he left to the priests as long as these did not conflict with his ambitions. He was deeply concerned, however, with what would happen to the land if the population acknowledged the appearance of the King-Messiah, and made efforts to install him as the head of the government. Jesus knew all of this. But he could not renounce his messianic claim. He had accepted the royal acclaim; he had exercised authority over Temple customs which had been sanctioned by tradition and the Roman-appointed priesthood; it was Pesach-time, the time of the Jewish Festival of Freedom—the traditional memorial of redemption from slavery—and he was by his own statement and the belief of his followers the "anointed" and the "looked for." He was caught in a web of irrevocable circumstances. He could not turn back! That he changed his mind later might

be inferred from the statement that the Gospel attributes
to him while on the cross in the words: "Eli, Eli, lamah
sabachtani," my God, my God, why hast thou forsaken me?"
(Mt. 27:46; Mk. 15:34).

I believe that up to this time, Jesus had a complete and
abiding faith in his own messiahship. At the last supper—
the "Sedar"—Jesus distributes the bread (Passover matzah),
drinks the Passover kosher wine and says: "Verily, I say unto
you, I will drink no more of the fruit of the vine until the
day when I drink it new in the Kingdom of Heaven." (Mt.
26:29; Mk. 14:25). At the end of the parable of the servants
we find this interesting passage: (Mt. 25:31) "But when the
son of man shall come in his glory and all the angels with
him, then shall he sit on the throne of his glory." At the
house of the high-priest and in the council, the high-priest
asked him whether he is "the Christ, the son of the Blessed?"
(Mk. 14:61-62; Lk. 22:69) And Jesus answered: "I am, and
ye shall see the son of man sitting on the right of power, and
coming in the clouds of heaven." When he was asked for a
sign to show that he performs miracles, he answered: (Jn.
2:19) "destroy this Temple, and in three days, I will raise it
up." The gospel writer, evidently disturbed by this answer,
states that "he spoke of the temple of his body." (Jn. 2:19).

Because of this deep conviction that he was the Son of God
and that he would usher in the "Kingdom of Heaven," I
have come to think that Jesus until the last, expected divine
intervention and some sudden heavenly miracle to prevent
the end that came to him. When he was arrested by the

Romans, one of the friends of Jesus drew a sword and cut off the ear of one of the servants of the high-priest. Jesus apparently resents this with the remark: "Thinkest thou that I cannot now pray to my Father, and He shall presently give me more than twelve legions of angels?" (Mt. 26:53). Now recall his quoting that very famous passage, the first verse of Psalm 22, but not in the same Hebrew words: "God, my God, why hast Thou forsaken me?" These were according to Matthew and Mark, his last words. If this is correct, Jesus waited until the very last moment for divine intervention, and only when he felt that he was dying, did he give up that idea.

Whether this conjecture is correct or not, the Sadducean priests felt that they had enough evidence against Jesus to hand him over to the Roman authorities. They were badly frightened, as indeed they had reason to be. At one of their council meetings the fate of Jesus was considered. According to one Gospel they discussed the danger, and one of their number asked: "What do we? For this man doeth many miracles. If we let him alone, all men will believe in him, and the Romans will come and take away both our place and our nation." And the high-priest Caiaphas said: "Ye know nothing at all. Nor do you consider that it is expedient for us that one man die for the people, and that the whole nation perish not." (Jn. 11:47-50). The illegal Sadducean court[1] delivered him to the Romans. In the sight of the Sadducean priests—for there were very few or none who were Pharisees —he had not only been guilty of blasphemy in his assuming the guise of King-Messiah, the Son of God; he had not only

91

endangered the peace and the welfare of the Judeans[2] by
the royal honors that he accepted from his followers; he was
not only an unlawful intruder upon age-old customs whereby
pilgrims were enabled to exchange foreign coins and thus
(Mk. 15:7; Lk. 23:19) purchase animals for their offerings,
which must have been an important item in the income of
the priesthood—a privilege which they long enjoyed; but he
would surely be the cause of another anti-Roman insurrection like that under Barabbas (Mk. 15:7; Lk. 23:19) which
had recently been put down. The Romans were alert and
watchful. Jesus had challenged the authority of the Rome-
appointed Sadducean officials, therefore the authority of
Rome. He had committed not only blasphemy, but treason as
well, and must be gotten[3] out of the way, so said the council
of the accusers (Jn. 11:48-50). Roman cruelty was nothing
new to the Judeans—and another incitement to it must be
scotched at all costs. This was the argument of the anti-Jesus
elements.

Jesus is brought before Pilate. The governor asks him "art
thou the king of the Jews?" Jesus answers, "thou sayest."
Pilate asks:[4] "Hearest thou not how many things they witness
against thee?" There was no answer. The story is substan-
tially the same in all the Gospels. Jesus' answer, "thou sayest," was doubtlessly interpreted by him as meaning, "thou
sayest, but *I* do not." We have a similar expression: "That's
what *you* say." But it means just the opposite. Surely, if
Pilate, who was one of the most barbarous and anti-Semitic
procurators that Rome ever sent to Palestine, would have
wanted to free Jesus, there was nothing in the world that

could have prevented him from doing so. The governorship of Pilate has gone down as one of the worst in Palestine Jewish history, and to believe that suddenly at the trial of Jesus, Pilate wanted to please the Jewish mob, is fantastic. In two of the Gospels, Pilate is made to ask the Jews which of two accused should he liberate, Jesus, "the king of the Jews," or Barabbas? (Mt. 27:17; Mk. 15:9). In Matthew, Pilate asks what should he do to "Jesus which is called the Christ?" "And they all answered 'let him be crucified'." (Vs. 22). This is the only instance that I can find in the history of the Jews of this period, when Pilate willingly regarded his Jewish subjects as of sufficient importance to be guided by their wishes! The truth of the matter is that the same fate that was meted out to every pseudo-messiah that made his appearance in these Roman days, was meted out to Jesus. For the Romans, the word "messiah" meant "king." The Jews were only being mocked by the Roman.

Pilate brings Jesus out, and says to the Jews: "Behold, your king!" Again, he asks, "shall I crucify your king?" "We have no king but Caesar," the "chief priests" answered. Then he delivers him to be crucified. (Mt. 27:26; Mk. 15:15). The superscription on the cross—over the head of Jesus, according to two of the Gospels, was: "This is the king of the Jews." (Mk. 15:26; Lk. 23:38). In John, the title was a little different: "Jesus of Nazareth, king of the Jews." (Jn. 19:19). Pilate regarded Jesus as a dangerous political rebel, a fomentor of rebellion and a danger to the power of Rome.

III.

Thus the Romans removed another of those Jewish patriots who believed that he was the long looked-for and eagerly-expected Messiah—deliverer and king. But he was killed by the Romans—not by the Jews, and was crucified according to Roman custom, by Roman soldiers and not by Jews.

Because of the popular wide-spread opinion that the Jews crucified Jesus, it is necessary to emphasize the fact that at this time, the Jews did not possess the right to inflict capital punishment, as correctly stated in the Gospel of John: "The Jews said unto him (Pilate), 'it is not lawful for us to put any man to death" (18:31). Nor was crucifixion a Jewish method of execution, even if they had had the legal right. When the Judean State had its independence and its Sanhedrin was the chief law-making body and had the right to inflict the death penalty—never crucifixion—the legal protection for the criminal was so effective that it was difficult to sentence one to death. At the time of Jesus, the power to inflict death was a purely Roman privilege, and the unjust and unhistorical information that the Jews killed Jesus, must be eradicated. Let us review in more detail the Gospel of John account of the crucifixion.

Jesus is brought before Pilate, whom the Gospel of John makes a very considerate and saintly man—one who is deeply sensitive to the wishes of his hated Jews. He has killed and crucified thousands, but in this case, his fountain of mercy is opened, and he listens to the voice of conscience which has been dormant or non-existent, where Jews were concerned, since the day he arived as procurator.

Let us then refresh our memory about this man whom the Gospels have portrayed as the innocent victim of Jewish obstinacy, Jewish blindness and Jewish cruelty.

He came to Judea about 26 of the present era. Like most of his predecessors, he expected to make himself rich at the expense of those whom he governed. This was a pattern for Roman officials, and he followed it. He spared no efforts to realize this ambition. He hated Jews, their religion and their laws. He mocked their religious beliefs, and persecuted, wounded, killed and crucified those who defended them. He went further than most of his predecessors in humiliating and crushing those who were loyal to their Jewish heritage.

Let me quote from Josephus (Bk. II, Ch. 1, Sec. 2ff): "Now Pilate who was sent as procurator into Judea, sent by night those images of Caesar that are called ensigns, into Jerusalem. This excited a very great tumult among the Jews . . . for those that were near them were astonished at the sight of them, as indications that their laws were trodden under foot; for the laws do not permit any sort of image to be brought into the city." This was their interpretation of the second commandment. "A vast number of people came zealously to Pilate at Caesarea and besought him to carry those ensigns out of Jerusalem to preserve their ancient laws inviolable; but upon Pilate's denial of the request, they fell prostrate upon the ground, and continued immovable for five days and as many nights."

"On the next day . . . Pilate gave a signal to the soldiers that they should encompass the Jews with their weapons . . . the Jews were under the utmost consternation at the unexpected sight. Pilate told them that they would be cut in pieces unless they would admit Caesar's images, and gave intimation to the soldiers to draw their naked swords. Hereupon the Jews . . . fell down, exposed their necks bare, and cried out that they were sooner ready to be slain than that their laws should be transgressed. Hereupon Pilate was greatly surprised and gave orders that the ensigns be carried out of Jerusalem."

"After this, he raised another disturbance, by expending the sacred treasure of the Temple which is called CORBAN, upon aqueducts. At this the multitude had indigation, and when Pilate came to Jerusalem they came about his tribunal and made a clamour at it. When he was apprized of this disturbance, he mixed his own soldiers in their armour with the multitude and ordered them to conceal themselves under the habits of private men, and not indeed, to use their swords, but with their staves to beat those that made clamour. . . . Now the Jews were so badly beaten, that many of them perished by the stripes they received and many of them perished as trodden to death by themselves."

Here is another incident from the governorship of this "good man" (Jos. Ant. Bk. XVIII, Ch. IV, Sec. 1): "But the nation of the Samaritans did not escape without tumults." There was a man "who had bid them to get together upon

Mt. Gerizim, which is by them looked upon as the most holy of all mountains, and who assured them that when they were come thither, he would show them those sacred vessels which Moses had put there. So . . . they came in a great multitude to go up to the mountain. But Pilate prevented their going up by seizing upon the roads with a great band of horsemen and footmen who fell upon those who were gotten together; some of them his men slew, others of them they put to flight, and took a great many alive; the principal of which, and also the most potent of those that fled away, Pilate ordered to be slain." These events do not, of course, take into consideration those many Jews who singly or in very small groups were killed or crucified by the procurator.

Philo of Alexandra thus quotes Agrippa I, in his "Embassy to Caius" (quoted in Klausner's "Jesus of Nazareth (p. 163) and referred to in Zeitlin's "Who Crucified Jesus"): "Pilate was cruel by nature and in his hard heartedness entirely lacking in remorse." His administration was marked by "bribes, vainglorious and insolent conduct, robbery, oppression, humiliations, men often sent to death untried, and incessant and unmitigated cruelty." This is the Pilate who so unctuously refuses to hand Jesus over to his soldiers, but finally gives way to the insistence of the "Jews who demand the crucifixion of Jesus."

The Gospel of John is more dramatic than the others. Pilate comes out from the judgment hall to ask the accusers of Jesus what accusation they had against him (18:29). They do not answer him directly, but inform the procurator that "if he were not a malefactor, they would not have delivered him unto thee!" A rather unexpected and tart reply from the minions of the governor to their boss! Then Pilate tells the accusers to take Jesus and judge him according to their law. They tell him that "it is not lawful for us to put any man to death" (Vs. 31). Pilate asks Jesus "art thou the king of the Jews?" Jesus does not answer directly and Pilate asks again, after Jesus explains that his "kingdom is not of this world." Then Pilate goes out "unto the Jews again, and says unto them, 'I find in him no fault'." Then comes Pilate's question again as to whether he should release Jesus, "King of the Jews," or Barabbas, who was accused of insurrection and murder, and the accusers cry (Vs. 40), "not this man, but Barabbas."

Pilate then has Jesus scourged, and brought out again, saying (19:4): "Behold I bring him forth again to you, that ye may know that I find no fault in him." Then why did he have him scourged if he were innocent? To please the Jews? Upon seeing him again, the "chief priests and officers cried out again, saying, 'crucify him, crucify him'." But still Pilate refuses. The Jews then accuse Jesus of blasphemy—"because he made himself the Son of God, and by our law, he ought to die." This frightened Pilate; just why, we are not told. Pilate is made to question Jesus again, and we are told that "from thence Pilate sought to release him; but (Vs. 12) the Jews cried out saying, 'if thou let this man go, thou art not Caesar's friend; whosoever maketh himself a king, speaketh against Caesar'." Once again Pilate asks, "shall I crucify your king?" Again comes the cry, "crucify him, we have no king but Caesar." That settled it for Pilate. Only after all of these "attempts to save Jesus," did Pilate hand him over to be crucified!

Anyone familiar with the imperiousness and the conceit of the Roman procurators, and with the contempt and almost universal disregard that they, and particularly Pilate, had for the Judeans, must be amused by this naive statement of the Gospel-writer which is intended to impress upon Pilate that he will not be "Caesar's friend" if he releases Jesus. For a group of Jews to tell the Roman procurator what his duty is, is to say the least, extraordinary! How little the writer of the Gospel knew about actual Roman-Jewish relations!

The Gospels as stated do not agree in several particulars. Matthew tells that the wife of Pilate advised her husband not to have anything to do with "that righteous man for I have suffered many things this day in a dream because of him" (Mt. 27:19). We are not told what the dream was. Mark informs us that Pilate wanting "to content the multitude released unto them Barabbas." It is most interesting that the Roman keeper of peace would, to please these particular Jews, liberate an insurrectionist who had in the course of the insurrection committed murder (Mk. 15:7), instead of crucifying him as had been the regular custom of Roman officials. We are also told: "Pilate took some water, washed his hands before the multitude, and said, 'I am innocent of the blood of this righteous man.'" It is revealing to see how this man who never hid his contempt and hatred for Jews and their practices, suddenly used a Jewish custom to persuade his minions that he was innocent. The Gospel writer remembered that it was customary for the elders of a Jewish city near which a person who had been slain was found, to wash their hands (Dt. 21:1-7) and say: "Our hands have not shed this blood, neither have our eyes seen it." This custom is also referred to in Psalms (26:6; 73:13) : "I will wash my hands in innocency. Surely in vain have I cleansed my heart, and washed my hands in innocency.". To have put these words into the mouth of Pilate to prove that he was innocent of the blood of Jesus, is as historically vicious an act as was the recording by the Gospel of a statement that never could have been made by the accusers of Jesus, simply because they did not have the authority to speak for all of the people: "Then answered all the people and said, 'His blood be on us and on our children'." (Mt. 27:25). This sentence, taken literally, has evoked as much bitterness and undeserved cruelty as any statement in the library of anti-Jewish literature. For it has made the whole Jewish people liable for something in which only a few—and those discredited—took part. It has been used as a justification for the injustice, persecution and pogromming and murder of literally millions of innocent people.

The tragic fact about the story of the crucifixion is that in spite of the disagreement about the event in the Gospels; in spite of the proven unhistorical references in the accounts; in spite of the evidence of Josephus and Philo regarding the character of Pontius Pilate; in spite of the manifest hypocrisy and insincerity of Pilate during the trial; in spite of the

Gospel evidence that Pilate as procurator had the right and could have released Jesus if he had really wanted to; in spite of the evidence that Pilate did hand Jesus over to his soldiers to be crucified—in spite of all of this the Christian world has accepted as true the account of his crucifixion, and has laid the blame upon Israel. It appears at times, that the Christian world does not care to know the real truth, or it fears that if the truth be known and believed, the inspiration of the Scriptures will be suspected, and faith in the Bible marred. This need not be so at all—for its truly religious teachings are eternal and will last as long as time itself.

The eminent Methodist clergyman of Chicago, Dr. George E. Fowler, has made the following, to my mind, correct observation:

"The Christian world has misinterpreted the account of the crucifixion. The truth must be impressed upon Christians everywhere. Certainly truth, wherever found, cannot invalidate the inspiration of the Scriptures nor mar faith in the Bible for its religious teachings are eternal and will last as long as time itself."

IV.

One leaves the description of the trial of Jesus with the impression that all the Jews wanted him crucified; that they came to the trial to demand the death of the "blasphemer"— and would not leave the praetorium or the procurator's residence where the trial took place, unless Pilate promised to crucify him. This is completely unhistorical. It is quite patent that many Jews could not get into the palace because of sheer numbers. In the second and more important place, the death and the trial of Jesus, as in fact the crucifixion, made practically no impression on the Judeans at the time they happened. But in order to make the Jews more barbarous and brutal, Pilate was made more considerate and more gentle. In fact one of the Church fathers—Tertullian—called him a "Christian" at heart! Either the statements ascribed to Pilate are right, and Pilate was a good man, or the Gospels are all wrong. Pontius Pilate was according to all historical sources quoted, one of the worst procurators and Jew-haters of ancient times. If the Gospel writers knew this, they managed to disguise it, and make the Jews the scapegoats. Pilate was recalled to Rome, in disgrace!

Prof. A. T. Olmstead, in his "Jesus" (p. 243) wrote: "The tragedy was ended. Jesus had endured atrocious suffering and was dead because he had excited the bitter hatred of the unprincipled high-priestly gang. Not a voice can be raised in their defense. Josephus had repeatedly and rightly blackened their reputation. Jewish fathers of a later generation remembered their names only to curse their rapacity and greed." This Christian scholar, Prof. Olmstead, was not the only one to cite Jewish sources which have condemned the prepetrators of the trial of Jesus. Dr. Klausner, in his "Jesus of Nazareth" (pp. 337-8) states: "It is interesting to note that the Talmud complains of the 'staves' and 'clubs' of the Boethusean High Priests including all infamous High

Priests (among them the Annas of the Gospels) from the time of Herod onwards." Two lines of a street ballad, he continues, run as follows: "Woe is me for the house of Boethus: Woe is me for their club! Woe is me for the house of Ishmael (ben Phiabi) : Woe is me for their fist! For they are the High Priests, and their sons are the treasurers; their sons-in-law are Temple officers and their servants beat the people with their staves."[1] Klausner continues: "There could scarcely be a more dreadful and hateful picture of the High Priests and their families. Their outstanding features were their clubs . . . staves, fists and secret denouncements. These were those who ordered Jesus' arrest and who conducted his preliminary examination. The Talmud hates them and regards them as enemies of the people whom they beat with their staves. The Gospels which are as full as the Talmud of suppressed hate against them, try to depict them as the agents of the Jewish people, and so blame the entire people for their acts. Hatred spoils sound judgment."

Students of the New Testament and New Testament times, are beginning to agree that one of the most tragic mistakes of Christian history, is the unfortunate attitude created by the story of the Passion of Jesus, which gives the impression that all the Jews of Judea and Jerusalem were involved in the trial and the crucifixion. The almost universal accusation of centuries that the Jews were "Christ-killers," and the indifferent and often friendly attitude of the Christian clergy to this accusation and the accusers, cost the Jewish people millions of lives. Within the last half century enlightened Christian scholarship has attempted, and has to some degree succeeded, in educating Christians to the truth of the fact that it was a small number of Sadducean High Priests, minions of the Roman procurator, and not the Jews as a whole, that turned Jesus over to the Roman authorities, because they were afraid that he would be the center of an insurrection against the Roman power, with terrifying results for the Jews.

It is not generally known that the Gospels do not agree in the details of those alleged events which they record. They differ about who came with Judas to arrest Jesus; they disagree on the day of the arrest, on just what was said at the trial by the representatives of the illegal Sanhedrin; and about the meaning of what Jesus answered Pilate, who was sublimated into an humble admirer of Jesus, instead of exposing what he was, a ruthless persecutor of the Jewish people to which Jesus by birth, by loyalty and by his death, belonged. Consideration of the mistakes, the contradictions and the inconsistencies in the narratives of the arrest and trial, is too large a matter for this volume. Those interested can find readable and historical expositions of the latest knowledge and research on the subject, in Klausner's "Jesus, His Life and Times;" Zeitlin's "Who Crucified Jesus;" and Pierre Van Paassen's "Why Jesus Died."

The High Priests and their subordinates were held responsible for order in Judea by the Romans who appointed them to office. It is understandable that they would get nervous about another messianic pretender. Since they had not the legal right to try political offenders, and they did want Jesus out of the way because they feared him, they shifted their base to a religious issue using also his alleged royal pretension. Here they had a right to arrest and try an offender, but not to inflict capital punishment. On the charge of blasphemy, they could try Jesus, and they did, and finding him guilty, could and did hand him over to the Romans. But to say, as the Gospels do, that THE JEWS did this, is just an historical and tragic inaccuracy.

It is true that Jesus differed from the Pharisees in several matters. He differed with regard to some aspects of the Sabbath; they did not believe that he was "Lord of the Sabbath"; he differed with them regarding fasting; with regard to washing the hands; he differed with them in his attitude towards sinners and publicans, and called them hypocrites. But never did Pharisaism interdict discussion. The Mishnah and the Talmudic writings and other literature which stemmed from them could never have been possible without discussion of the differences. Hundreds of rabbis and students differed with each other—practically all Pharisees—yet we have no death penalties for these differences even during the time when the Sanhedrin could have inflicted them. The alleged blasphemy of Jesus was a forced interpretation of his words—in order to make it possible for the High Priestly clique to bring the object of their fear before Pilate, who they knew would get him out of the way. For to Pilate, Jesus was just another of those accursed Jewish Galilean fanatics who believed that he had been selected by God to be what Pilate had put on the cross: "Jesus of Nazareth, King of the Jews."

In the accounts of the arrest and trial, the Gospel writers

again showed they were writing not for history, but for the growing Christian religion which did not spread too quickly among Jews. And since Judaism and nascent Christianity were not at peace while the evangelists were editing their stories, it did not hurt their consciences to put the Jews—all the Jews—in as bad a light as they could, under the circumstances. Unfortunately the Christian world has accepted the unhistorical representations, to the infinite sorrow of the Children of Israel!

Prof. Joseph Klausner, in his "Jesus of Nazareth" (p. 151), says: "The Sanhedrin, the true supreme authority of the Jewish people, was in Herod's time virtually non-existent. It was suffered to deal only with unimportant religious matters, whereas in civil matters it was compelled to submit to the dictation of the tyrant. The high priests he changed as he might have changed clothes. We have seen that at that time Jews could not pass sentence of death (John 18:31): 'It is not lawful for us to put any man to death,' at least not in a case affecting a Messiah, i. e., a political question (p. 345). . . . It is certain that the priests did not see in Jesus anything more than an ordinary rebel. They therefore bound Jesus and brought him to Pilate. Certain of the priestly party went with him, and explained to Pilate that the Sanhedrin had condemned Jesus for assuming the role of Messiah, i. e., King of the Jews; such was all the meaning that 'Messiah' could convey to Pilate the Roman (p. 348). A few only of the priestly caste had condemned Jesus to death and given him up to Pilate, primarily because of their dread of the same

Pilate, and only incidentally because of their annoyance at the 'cleansing of the Temple' and because Jesus 'mocked' at the words of the wise, and spoke ill of the Temple; and what was more serious, because of his blasphemy in thinking himself 'the Son of man coming with the clouds of heaven' who should sit at the right hand of God. Through fear of the Roman tyrant, those who were then the chief men among the Jews delivered up Jesus to this tyrant. No Jew took any further part in the actual trial and crucifixion: Pilate the 'man of blood' was responsible for the rest." (p. 349). To say that the 'Jews' crucified Jesus or that they were even responsible for his death by crucifixion, is grossly untrue. The Jews as a nation, were far less guilty of the death of Jesus than the Greeks as a nation were guilty of the death of Socrates; but who would now think of avenging the blood of Socrates the Greek upon his countrymen, the present Greek race? Yet for these nineteen hundred years past, the world has gone on avenging the blood of Jesus the Jew, upon his countrymen, the Jews, who still go on paying the penalty...."

Prof. Solomon Zeitlin in his "Who Crucified Jesus" (p. 81-82), says: "Prior to the conquest of Judea, if the ruler had a case against any individual, he summoned the political Sanhedrin to pass judgment upon him; then the ruler carried out the punishment of the culprit. With the conquest of the country by the Romans, the procurator assumed entire authority of the legal procedure. He passed judgment and inflicted punishment on the accused charged with seditious acts against the state. The high priests were appointed by the procurator. They were men who the authorities knew would execute their policies. To them the procurator entrusted the task of enforcing political and social order in Judea. The high priests were responsible to the Romans for the tranquility of their country. It was their duty to hunt out the malcontents, the rebels against the state, and to report them to the Roman officials. Dependent on the Roman procurator, they proved obedient servants to their masters. Watchdogs of the Roman imperialism, some of them were even ready to exterminate Jews who raised arms against their conquerors.

"The high priests were reduced to agents of the procurator. They arrested those considered a menace to the state, summoned a Sanhedrin before which they presented the evidence in the case for the prosecutor; then the prosecutor passed judgment on the convicted and carried out the judgment. Thus we may describe some of the high priests in the time of Jesus as being like 'Quislings' of our own troublesome days.

"A superficial reading of the story of the Passion gives the impression that the Jews were responsible for the crucifixion of Jesus (p. 171). Jesus was crucified as the king of the Jews. The Jewish religious Sanhedrin and the Jewish people had nothing to do with the trial of Jesus. The high priest who actually delivered Jesus to the Roman authorities either was compelled to do so to save himself so as not to be accused of being an accessory to the rebels; or most likely, Caiaphas the high priest, played the role of a Quisling who proved ready to sell out Judea to the Romans for personal gain."

JESUS, PILATE AND PAUL

Pierre Van Paassen, an American minister, in his "Why Jesus Died (p. 149), says: "Dr. Guignebert, the greatest authority on the life and times of Jesus, feels certain that the Jewish authorities were not involved in the matter (arrest and trial of Jesus). He leans to the view that the 'arresting party was made up of self-appointed vigilantes, tipsters, stool pigeons, and other social riffraff of that kind'." There doubtless is some truth in this position since the Gospels do not establish clearly the identity of the arresting party. Matthew (26:47) says: "And while he yet spake, Judas, one of the twelve, came and with him a great multitude with swords and staves, from the chief priests and the elders of the people." Mark (14:43) states: "And straightaway, while yet he spake, cometh Judas, one of the twelve, and with a multitude with swords and staves, from the chief priests and the scribes and the elders." Luke has it (22:47): "While he yet spake, behold a multitude, and he that was called Judas, one of the twelve, went before them and he drew unto Jesus to kiss him." The impression in these quotations is that the Jewish people were responsible for both the betrayal and the arrest, and of course, the crucifixion. And that impression is still dominant among millions of Christians!

Van Paassen also quotes the following from Prof. Alfred Loisy (p. 149), one of the greatest Catholic New Testament commentators, who was later expelled from the Church: "If Jesus was crucified, he was sentenced by and executed by the Roman authorities as a seditious person. A judgment by the Sanhedrin had to be concocted, as well as a condemnation by the same judicial body on the grounds of alleged preten-

109

sions by Jesus of being the Son of God, that is to say a divine quality which the Galilean prophet did not claim for himself but which was claimed for him many years after his death by the makers of the Christian mystery religion. Must we repeat again, that the New Testament texts do not deal with historical facts but with catechesis and apologetics."

Let it be repeated until all know it—not the Jews—but the Romans killed Jesus!

III.

From Jesus to the Rise of Paul

I.

THE CRUCIFIXION AND death of Jesus stunned his disciples and filled them with consternation. For a time they did not know what to do. That the Romans had removed their leader from the field of human activity, there was no doubt. But there were those who believed in some sort of a divine Messiah. Students disagree as to whether Jesus considered himself the expected Messiah or not, but it is very evident that after the first shock was over, his disciples did. The expectations of Israel's liberation which they had hoped Jesus would bring about, were blasted, but it was impossible for them to believe that his death was the end either for him or for them. Moreover, according to Christian tradition, Jesus appeared to Mary Magdalene and Mary the mother of James—the Gospels differ in the accounts of those who were present—to Peter and to the eleven; then to James, to 500 others and after his purported ascension, to Paul. There is no agreement in the accounts of the appearances. His early disciples recalled his life, his teachings, and his death which became to them the most important event of his life. They dedicated themselves to the spreading of his teachings and to the story of his death and ascension. We find no evidence that Jesus' teachings included those later Pauline doctrines which began to be the real marks of the nascent Christianity, as differentiated from Judaism.

The followers of Jesus increased[1] as they spread the message of his life and their meaning of his death and resurrection. Not only were some Jews impressed with these, but those Gentiles who lived outside of Jerusalem came under their influence. Later knowledge about him spread into the cities along the Jordan and into the Mediterranean region. As the accounts of his life were repeated, they began to be modified in accordance with the training and the beliefs and cultures of those who heard them. Not too long after his death, his Gentile followers outnumbered those who had been born Jews, and separated completely from the Jewish community.

Among the non-Palestinian Jews who had come to Jerusalem and had heard about Jesus, was one Saul of Tarsus, later known as Paul. In Jerusalem he joined those who were opposed to the messianic-doctrines which the disciples of Jesus preached. Tradition says that he was one of those who helped in the stoning of Stephen who was a chief advocate of the messiahship of Jesus. He was a man of frail health, subject to mental seizures, and is thought by many to have been an epileptic.

Paul heard of the increase in numbers of the followers of Jesus and their teachings, if indeed he had not become familiar with them, and decided to go to Damascus which had become a center of the sect, to battle against them. Up to this time Paul had been an ardent Jew. He called himself a "Hebrew of the Hebrews," and according to one source, asserted that he had gone to Jerusalem to sit at the feet of Gamaliel who was the head of the Sanhedrin. He was, according to his own story, a strict, observing Jew. There is no evidence in the Jewish contemporary writings that he was a student of Gamaliel.

As Paul nears Damascus on his way from Jerusalem, he has a vision. As told in (Acts 22:6) he sees a sudden great light from heaven, and falls prostrate to the ground. He hears a voice saying, "Saul, Saul, why persecutest thou me?" And Saul asks, "Who art thou, Lord?" The answer comes, "I am Jesus of Nazareth whom thou persecutest." And Paul or Saul asks, "What shall I do? And the Lord said unto me: 'Arise and go to Damascus, and there it shall be told thee which things are appointed for thee to do'."

Paul goes to Damascus. The vision had had so terrifying an effect upon him, that he was blinded for three days during which time he neither ate nor drank. (Acts 9:9). The appearance of him who was in life the man Jesus, now resurrected as Christ, was the effective dramatization of the resurrected-savior-god teachings of the mystery religions[2] with which he was familiar in his native Tarsus. He himself now was the recipient of grace and salvation from the resurrected-savior-god, Christ, about whom he would go to the synagogues to preach (9:20). During these days of mental and physical strain, he must have become convinced of the effectiveness of Gentile mystery religions in the lives of their devotees.

We have no evidence that he ever considered adopting any of them, tho references in his letters indicate that he was friendly to them. If he had ever in moments of doubt considered the doctrines in regard to his own salvation and doubted them, the effect of this vision certainly was sure to dispel the doubt and change his whole life in favor of the Jewish "mystery."

It was this vision then, that removed whatever hesitancy Paul may have entertained about the truth of the doctrine of the dying and resurrected god who alone could bring him salvation. Jesus of Nazareth who had been crucified in Jerusalem was to him that savior, now sitting in Heaven at the right-hand of God, and fulfilling his office as redeemer of that portion of mankind that accepts him as the Son of God. Paul believed that Jesus had lived, tho he had not seen him in the flesh. The vision now verified this for him. Jesus appears to him now in glory to enlist him in the work of evangelization. Paul decides that his mission was to convert the world to the doctrine that he who was Jesus in life on earth, has been by his resurrection, transformed into the heavenly Christ, the divine redeemer, the Son of God. Paul believed that the Passion of Jesus had proved him to be the expected Messiah and conferred upon him eternal glory and Lordship; that he is the Son whom God loved, who came on earth to die that men may be saved, and who was foretold in Scripture. Prof. Glover[3] sums it up thus: "The whole of Paul's subsequent thought is based on the truth of the Resurrection, on Christ working in the power of an infinite life, a working whereby he is able to 'subdue all things unto himself,' 'declared to be the Son of God with power, according to the spirit of holiness, by the resurrection from the dead.' Jesus from that moment is for Paul, a divine being, and the identity is patent of the historical Jesus and the Risen Christ."

II.

Paul and the Mystery Cults

Thus far, nothing has been said about the meaning or the significance of Paul's chief contribution to Christianity, namely, the concept of salvation thru the "risen Christ," which is the main rock upon which Judaism and Christianity split. For many people there is no difference between "Jesus" and "Christ." But these two words have altogether different significations, depending upon the contexts in which they are used. Jesus is the name of a great personality who walked among men, lived and died. Christ, is the title applied by Paul, to this personality after his death, and describes him as the means thru which salvation and future life are secured by those who accept him as the sacrificial lamb, the only begotten son of God, sent on earth to be the sacrificial atonement for their sins; and their savior and redeemer as taught in the Gospels and by Paul of Tarsus.

It might be interesting to indicate here how Saul or Paul,

a Hellenistic Jew, probably developed his Christological ideas.

For several centuries before the Christian era, religious movements known as mystery cults, had been spreading over Asia Minor.[1] These came largely from Egypt, Persia and Mesopotamia. They promised their devotees a divine favor which was otherwise unattainable, peace in this world and eternal salvation in the next. Cumont[2] tells us that "Oriental mysteries offered their votaries radiant prospectives of eternal happiness. The aim was the attainment of the sovereign good in the life hereafter instead of in this world, as Greek philosophy had taught. Existence in this life was regarded as a preparation for a sanctified life, as a trial, whose outcome was to be either everlasting happiness or everlasting pain." Frazer echoes this in the words: "The entire center of gravity was shifted from the present to the future."[3]

In the teachings of the mystery religions, the state of the future life—the salvation of the soul—became the greatest human concern. Purification and redemption by a god, were the means of achieving this salvation, but certain ceremonies had to be performed. These dealt with the death and resurrection of the particular god around whom the cult was built. The worship of Tammuz, Sabazius, Dionysus, Osiris, Attis and Adonis, savior-gods, whose births were miraculous and whose mothers, in some cases were virgins, had struck deep root over the whole Mediterranean area. Sometimes a god was the physical father. As a matter of fact, a number of ancient "heroes" were born of a mortal mother and a divine father; so Aratus of Sicyon, a Greek statesman of the third century; so Alexander the Great of Macedon; so Augustus Caesar, and it was even said of Scipio the Elder! It is well known that emperor-worship was a belief that the emperors were descended from gods. And it should not be forgotten that one of the major issues in the Maccabean struggle was the insistence of the Emperor Antiochus Epiphanes and his image was to receive obeisance; but the Judeans refused to bow down to it.

A large number of Jewish colonies was scattered in Asia Minor. Paganism and Judaism influenced each other in the same manner that Judaism and Christianity influence each other today. Hebrew and Greek usages and Jewish and Pagan philosophies were intermixed. The Hellenistic world was an important center of the dominant cults. Here, in what is now Turkey, but what was anciently the district of Cilicia in Syria, about twelve miles from the Mediterranean, was a city called Tarsus. It was noted for its safe harbor, its commerce in textile products, and for its schools of rhetoric which made it an intellectual center. In this city lived one Saul, later Paul and then St. Paul. If the accounts of his education and travel are true, he was a man of some culture. The only account of Paul that we have outside of the New Testament, is an unauthenticated work called "The Acts of Paul and Thekla," of uncertain date. It is placed as early as the second century and not later than the fifth. Paul was familiar with the mystery cults as indicated in his letters, and he had a knowledge of Judaism, tho he does not seem to have been well-versed in Hebrew. This is evidenced by the quotations in his writings which are all from the Septuagint,[4] the Greek translation of the Old Testament, and not from the Hebrew version.

Tho he calls himself a "Hebrew of the Hebrews," he could hardly escape the influence of Hellenistic culture and civilization in as deeply an assimilationist atmosphere as existed in Tarsus. We are told by Prof. William Ramsay that Tarsus was peculiarly "successful in producing an amalgamated society in which Oriental society and Occidental spirit in unison, attained in some degrees to a higher plane of thought and action." Paul remained in Tarsus thruout his early and later youth. He attests to the influence which the Hellenistic civilization had on him, with perhaps particular reference to the mystery religions and stoicism, by this statement (Ro. 1:14) : "I am debtor to the Greeks and Barbarians, both to the wise and the unwise." There is a strong similarity between the modern diaspora Jew and this non-Palestinian brother of nineteen centuries ago in the result of the impact of their contemporary cultures upon them. The modern Jew who has assimilated to a large extent the culture of his country, is by virtue of that assimilation less ritually observant than the pious Jew who has not become as completely assimilated. Progressive civilization has its effect upon religion and theology as well as upon other elements of contemporary culture. Reform Judaism, for instance, is an example of that form of Judaism which adjusts itself to contemporary customs and forms of life, as long as these do not violate the basic doctrines of the faith.

Some Jews born of Jewish parents observe very little of

Judaism, and some deny the validity of religion altogether.
Yet whenever occasion demands it, they loudly proclaim
that "they are proud" of being Jews. The protestation that
"I am a Hebrew of Hebrews" that Paul uttered, may have
been applicable to his early life when he had his Jewish
religious practices in mind, but surely could not apply to
his later years. There are many Jews today, who maintain
that "once a Jew, always a Jew." There are some who have
joined Christian churches, but still regard themselves as Jews.
Every once in a while, some Christian minister tells me that
he has a "Jewish" family who joined his church. Many do
not yet consider that the only difference between Terah the
father of Abraham, and Abraham himself, was that the former was a pagan worshipper of idols, while Abraham had a
vision of the true One and only God. I believe that Paul
may have referred to his people, and used the word "Hebrew" to designate it, rather than to their religion.

There is no doubt that after years of life and observation
in Tarsus, Paul became convinced, as were the devotees of
the mystery cults, that man's most important concern is his
fate after death. That salvation is the supreme goal of the
human being, was their insistence, and whatever militated
against its achievement must be changed or ignored. This
life is but a "preparation." Perhaps he knew of the saying
of some rabbis, incorporated in later Jewish literature, "that
this life is but a vestibule to the life to come." But the rabbis
of course had no notion that a redeemer or savior in the
person of Christ was needed to bring about eternal bliss for
those who entered eternal life from the "vestibule." God was

their redeemer in this life and in any other. Paul did not overlook the importance of human existence, but this life to him, as to his contemporary devotees of the mysteries, was after all only the bud to open into full bloom in the after-life. Because of this conviction his mind was directed towards the formation of a plan which would insure for those who accepted it, peace in this world and everlasting salvation in the new world which according to Jesus, was about to dawn. To achieve this, Paul's "risen Christ" concept of the dying and resurrected god — the central teaching of the mystery cults, was enunciated.

To quote Case:[5] "The religion with which Paul endeavored to win the Gentile world preserved a large number of Jewish characteristics, but it also contained many new features serving to meet certain religious demands distinctive of the Graeco-Roman world in Paul's day. He kept the Jewish figure of the Messiah, but he presented him in a form which transcended that of the Roman emperor who was being worshipped as savior, Lord, son of God, and God. Christianity was the new imperial religion which held out to believers not merely temporary civic blessings, but membership in an eternal divine kingdom. . . . In this latter respect Paul was more closely akin to the ideal of the contemporary mystery-religions. In his pictorial presentation of the crucified Messiah he was able to stage a more vivid and effective mystery-drama, he believed, than that which one witnessed in the rites of any other cult. His religion—like the other mysteries, but more effectively in the belief of the Christians—supplied to initiates the privileges of union with the dying and rising

Savior who ultimately would confer upon his followers a life of immortal blessedness." In another connection, Prof. Case asks:[6] "On the whole would it not be more truly descriptive of Paul's attitude to call his religion a 'Christ' (Messiah) cult, rather than a 'Lord' (Kyrios) cult?" In these two passages one finds the answer, in short form, to the question why the Jews did not accept Pauline Christianity. They wanted neither a mystery religion, nor an after-death messianic cult, nor any kind of a new faith.

This conception of Paul must have been burning itself into his consciousness for many years. He was well enough acquainted with the teachings of Judaism to know that any doctrine of a divine savior other than God, ran contrary to general Jewish belief and thinking. The followers of some of the apocalyptists had some vague ideas about a semidivine heavenly redeemer, but these found little credence. He knew, doubtless, that Judaism would not brook the sharing of the divine power by God, with anyone or anything. He must have known that the very "watchword" of Judaism was, as it is now (Dt. 6:4), "Hear, O Israel, the Lord our God the Lord is One," and corollary to it, "there is none like unto Him." He must have spent many thoughtful moments on the problem that confronted him, namely, how to present the concept of his Lord and Savior after death, in a way which would meet the objections of those who held the absolute one God idea and maintained that God alone is the Redeemer here and hereafter.

We have no record of Paul's thinking along these lines,

before the vision near Damascus. Evidently he felt that there was no need to record his thoughts on these matters. His almost ferocious persecution of the followers of Jesus before that call, was no doubt an unconscious reaction against his subconscious, growing beliefs. The severity of his inner conflict could have brought on his collapse and the vision. Prof. T. R. Glover[7] has some interesting comments on the situation: "It has already been suggested that he (Paul) had also to fight against the consequences of long familiarity with the Hellenistic world; here too, he was divided against himself and (as befalls men in such a state) he was more violent on one side because he wished to be on both sides. A youth passed in Gentile surroundings, a manhood devoted to work among Gentiles, hang together; and somewhere under the surface, it is hardly overbold to surmise that a lifetime's instinct was making a fierce struggle against the theory of a season—his humanism against his tribalism; and the latter betrays the uneasiness of its temporary triumph by its violence. We can imagine him perplexed in the extreme—growing angry with himself and as a result more violent, as if to force himself away from distasteful hypotheses or doubts, and more savage with his work of persecution."

I do not think that Paul took lightly, the contradiction between the conception of the uniqueness of the Jewish doctrine that God alone was the Redeemer and Savior of His children, and that of the mystery religions which regarded other gods as redeemers and saviors. Paul was honest in his desire to bring about salvation, first for his fellow-Jews, and when that became impossible for him, for the Gentiles. The desire in his mind to bring his own people to his way of thinking and then the realization that he could not do it, must have been a terrific blow to him. It was probably no mean decision for him to have turned largely away from the Jews to the Gentiles.

If it is true that Paul passed most of his youth among Gentiles; if it is true that in Tarsus mystery religions flourished, and Prof. Case[8] tells us that the "cult of Mithra had become so firmly established in Cilicia that Tarsus continued to worship him down to the end of the imperial period"— if it is further true that in the Graeco-Roman world, in the time of Paul "the human spirit conscious of its frailty and helpless at the loss of older sanctions, eagerly turned toward those cults which offered a personal salvation based upon a divine redemptive transaction,"[9] and if it is true—and I think that it is—that Paul could not find in his conception of Judaism, a formula for a blessed existence after death thru the redemption by a dying and resurrected god as was the case in the mystery cults—if all of this is true—it follows that Paul arrived at a syncretism in which he took the mortal Jesus, and transformed him into the dying and resurrected Savior—God, Christ. Prof. Riddle[10] gives a correct and succinct summary: "Appeal to gentile influence is often made to account for the difference between Paul's religion and the religion of other Jews. For example, the central place given Jesus' death and his life after death was in general agreement with the cult story of many a pagan religion. Paul taught that the believer in a mystical sense died with Christ, and when he was baptized he was figuratively buried with Christ, and that in the same mystical manner he was raised with Christ from among the dead, and was afterward in spiritual union with Christ. This secured for the believer the benefits of Christ's triumph over death. Obviously this approximates the substance of the typical cult myth and some of its ceremonies. It is thought that many features in Paul's religion were due to the influence of the mystery religions." While this Pauline doctrine, as noted, had some slight similarity to some of the Jewish apocalyptic mysticisms, it could find no lodgement in the minds of Jews generally. They therefore rejected the Pauline cult—as they rejected other elements foreign and antagonistic to Judaism.[11]

III.

Jewish and Pauline Conceptions of God

Most Westerners accept the belief in the unity of God. Monotheism, the doctrine that there is only one God, is the common conception of God except among those who call themselves agnostics or atheists. There is no quarrel about this primary concept of God among professing Jews, Christians and Muslims. There is however, a difference of interpretation as to the "oneness" and the "uniqueness" of God. It is this difference in interpretation of this teaching between Jews and Christians that has brought about the basis of the

theological conflict between Judaism and Pauline Christianity.[1] A man who asks for "grace and peace" not only from "God our Father, but also from our Lord Jesus Christ," must regard Christ as co-equal with God; however carefully the formulae distinguishing his unique nature from that of God may be worded, the practical faith of Paul and his congregations expects no less from Christ than from God—guidance, help and salvation. Christians' prayers as well as praises are offered to Him. As compared with the preaching of Jesus, this was a complete innovation. The phrase "in the Name of the Father, and the Son and the Holy Ghost," would sound as foreign to the Judaism of Jesus, as it did ages ago to his fellow-Jews and as it does to Jews today. Judaism did not and cannot accept the doctrine of the "only begotten Son of God" (Jn. 3:16). The Jewish[2] concept will not permit the possibility of God being able to divide Himself so that there can be "an only begotten Son," who may be a human being for a time, and then transformed into the "risen Christ" (Jn. 1:14; 3:16; Ro. 4:24), etc.

The one outstanding characteristic of Judaism thruout all of its history has been ethical monotheism—the belief in one, indivisible, omnipotent, just God. The Jewish conception of its God rejects any interpretation which violates the concept of the uniqueness and indivisibility of the Deity. Our "God is One, and there is no God like unto our God" has been the battle-cry of Judaism thruout the ages. The Jewish God does not share His power or His glory or His essence with anyone else. He is a spiritual Being without shape and without form, who is the sole Redeemer and Savior of mankind.

He is One, and because of His unique nature He cannot be two or three or many. His unity implies a cosmic order in which there is a harmonious interworking of God's laws of nature. This implies order in the realm of natural law and harmony in the realm of human intercourse.

God, not Jesus Christ, is the Creator of the Universe, tho man, by following what we are told are the wishes of God, can be partners with Him both in the realm of human affairs and in nature. God is one—our Father, and as such, the head of the brotherhood of human beings. This office none can share with Him. He works and moves and directs the universe here and hereafter—and this direction none can share with him. He is not according to Judaism, a far-off being who created the world and watches it from some far-away post. He is the Father of mankind, the Creator of the world, and the Rock and Support of His children. He is the First Cause of the universe, and this primacy He does not share with anyone else. Nature declares the glory of God, and this glory is not shared with anyone else. God cannot be likened to anyone or compared with anyone—and this uniqueness cannot be divided with anyone. None can share His rulership in this world or any other. He was first and will be last. He is a jealous God at times, but is ever merciful and gracious (Ex. 34:6) (Nu. 14:18-19), long suffering and abundant in goodness and truth; in fact He is Truth. He is the ever-ruling King and His throne is not shared by anyone. "Thine O Lord, is the greatness and the power and the glory, and the victory and the majesty; for all that is in heaven and in the earth is Thine; Thine is the kingdom, O Lord, and

Thou art exalted as head above all. Both riches and honor come from Thee and Thou rulest over all; in Thy hand are power and might." (1 Ch. 29:11-12). God is holy, and this holiness is uniquely His.

To sum up: For Judaism, past and present, God is the one unique Unity, indivisible, omniscient, omnipotent, spiritual, formless; the universal Father of humankind, transcending all in wisdom and power. All human beings are equally His children. By virtue of His unique nature, He cannot have one particular son or favorite, as could the ancient gods and goddesses or those of the mystery cults. He cannot share His unique divinity with anyone, and were He to assume human form, He would no longer be infinite and shapeless—but limited in space and in extension,[3] and therefore not God! To believe that God is a spirit, and then to believe, too, that Christ[4] sits at His right in heaven with Him (Ro. 8:34; 14:9: Eph. 1:20), etc., is to the Jewish mind, a patent contradiction. "Paul[5] articulated a view in which the redemptive work of Christ was absolutely cosmic in scope. That this view elevated Jesus in Paul's estimation, to a point where he was hardly less than God was an inevitable implication. But Paul was not conscious apparently, that this involved essential modification of the Jewish dogma of God's unity." The ancient Jew could not go along with Tertullion in his statement "credo quia absurdum est"—"I believe it (in the Trinity) because it is irrational"—contrary to common reason. Neither can the modern Jew. The divisibility of the God-head, the Trinity or the mystery of the Triune, the Father, Son and Holy Ghost—was and is impossible for a professor of Judaism. That many Jews anciently and now do believe in some "irrational" things does not change the matter.

Jews cannot believe that God came to earth in the person of Jesus, thus changing Himself into a human being, with the feelings, the qualities, the weaknesses, the instincts and the limitations of a mortal. All of this is foreign to the Jewish teaching that God is eternal, incorporeal and indivisible. While it is true that the Old Testament uses such phrases as "it repented God," "jealous God," the "finger of God," and similar ones, Jewish tradition accepts these only as expressions through which a human being can grasp what we believe to be divine attributes.[6] These expressions are called "anthropomorphisms,"[7] and are used figuratively. There were and there are Jews who conceive of God as a sort of sublimated human being, but this is not the classic Jewish conception of God. "Thou canst not see My face, for no man can see My face and live," said God to Moses. (Ex. 33:20). This still holds. A divided God with part of Him in heaven and part on earth or at His side in heaven, cannot be accepted. "Hear, O Israel, the Lord our God, the Lord is One," has always been the shibboleth of Judaism. Jesus could not be a part of God either on earth as a mortal or as Christ in heaven. It is not too difficult to see then, that when Paul said (I Cor. 8:6) : "But to us there is but one God, the Father, of whom are all things, and we in him, and one Lord Jesus Christ by whom are all things made, and we by him," it was quite confusing to his Jewish coreligionists. There are many similar passages. The English word "Lord" is a translation of the Greek "Kurios" and of the Hebrew word "Yahveh," the Supreme Being, God. Paul utilized the word "Lord" in the Greek, and applied it to Jesus and the risen Christ. To the Jew who heard this, this question must have occurred: "Who is the Lord God? Jesus Christ or Yahveh?" Says Case:[8] "Christians are those who call upon the name of our Lord Jesus Christ (I Cor. 1:2). Since God has temporarily committed all authority unto the risen Jesus, he is Lord of all." Again Case: "Paul uses the word 'Kurios' alone, referring to Jesus (tho whether used of Jesus or of God cannot always be positively decided) 139 times."

Riddle and Hutson in their very valuable volume, tell us:[9] Paul "believed that Jesus was God's son, God's anointed —the Messiah. Significantly, Paul also applied to Jesus the familiar term of Gentile cults; Jesus was his Lord." "For Paul, Jesus was the 'Lord,' the name given to adepts of Serapis."[10] But these adepts did not have the knowledge of "Lord God Yahveh" and knew little or nothing about the Jewish belief, and thus were not confused. To a Jew, "Grace be unto you and peace, from God our Father and from the Lord Jesus Christ," meant simply nothing. Similarly confusing is (I Cor. 1:9): "God is faithful, by whom ye are called unto the fellowship of His Son, Jesus Christ our Lord." The statement (Phil. 2:9 ff): "Wherefore God hath exalted Him and given him a name that is above every name in order that in the name of Jesus every knee should bow, of things in heaven, in earth and under the earth, and that every tongue should confess that Jesus Christ is Lord, to the glory of God the Father"—this statement sounded pretty foreign and revolutionary to a Jew who remembered the Eighth Psalm:

"O Lord our God, how glorious is Thy name in all the
   earth!
Whose majesty is rehearsed above the heavens.
When I behold Thy heavens, the work of Thy fingers,
The moon and the stars which Thou hast established,
What is man that Thou art mindful of him,
And the son of man that Thou thinkest of him?
Yet hast Thou made him but little lower than the angels
And hast crowned him with glory and honor.
Thou hast made him to have dominion over the works
   of Thy hands,
Thou hast put all things under his feet.
Sheep and oxen all of them, yea and the beasts of the field,
The fowl of the air and fish of the seas!
O Lord our God,
How glorious is Thy name in all the earth!"[4]

Paul's conception of God could not under any circumstances win the approval of the Jews. But the mystery cults had prepared both Paul and his Gentile contemporaries for its acceptance. Pauline Christianity spread so quickly among the Gentiles of Asia Minor because it was a synthesis of mystery-religion and Greek ethics.

IV.

The Jewish Concept of a Future Life

The Hebrews, like other ancient peoples, had as noted above, a vague belief in some kind of a future life, that is to say, a life after death and beyond the grave. With other Semitic groups, they believed that the dead continue their existence in what the Bible calls Sheol, a place in the underworld, inhabited by shadowy ghosts, leading a dull, colorless existence without a clear consciousness, and without any thought of awakening to a better life sometimes. Thruout the Bible there is no ethical idea involved in life after death, nor is there any mention made of the nether world as a place of divine judgment. There must have been however, some thought of everlasting life at the root of the stories of the translation of Enoch and Elijah to heaven with God. They believed in some kind of survival, in a land of no return, of eternal silence and oblivion. But it is certain that there was a progressive change in belief in regard to reward and punishment because the very favoritism shown to Enoch and Elijah, was due to their saintliness. Here lies the beginning of the later concept of reward and punishment. Later, the Book of Job and some of the Psalms call Sheol the "king of terrors" who ruled over the dead. And a Psalmist says: "God will redeem my soul from the power of the nether-world, for He shall receive me" (Ps. 49:15) . There is no intimation as to what that "power" was.

Says Dr. Kohler[1] in his "Jewish Theology: "Biblical Judaism evinced such a powerful impetus toward a complete and
blissful life with God, that the center and purpose of existence would not be transferred to the hereafter as in other
systems of belief, but was found in the desire to work out
the life here on earth to its fullest possible development."
This is true of the prophetic as well as of the wisdom literature. Nowhere in these is there definite mention of after-life.
Whatever is to be achieved in the direction of goodness and
godliness, is to take place in this world. The nether world—
that is the world after death—cannot praise God for in Sheol
it evidently does not know God" (Is. 38:18-19). "For the
nether world cannot praise Thee; death cannot celebrate
Thee. The living, the living, he shall praise Thee, as I
do this day." The task of the commandments and statutes
of Moses, and of the discourses of the prophets, of the songs
of the Psalmists and the sayings of the Proverbs, was to
educate the Jew and persuade him to give himself up to the
service of his God, by a life in this world that would follow
His will, summed up in Leviticus, "Holy shall ye be, for holy
am I the Lord your God." (Lev. 19:1) and by Isaiah (60:18-
21): "Violence shall no more be heard in thy land, wasting
nor destruction within thy borders . . . thy people also shall
be all righteous, they shall inherit the land forever . . . that
I may be glorified."

Because of the insistence of ethical conduct and its reward
in this world believed in earlier Israel, there was no need
for developing the thought of reward and punishment in
another world. This however did come, as the Jews came

in contact with their neighbors. While there are some passages that indicate a belief in the future world, they are of
later composition. While some verses in the Book of Job
have been interpreted as referring to a life after death, there
are at least two long passages which deny it. The reader is
referred to Job (7:8-10; 21 and 14:10-22). The rule of the
nether world by Sheol was gradually transferred to God, and
a belief began to develop that if God were the God of the
entire Universe, He was also the God of the underworld.
And if this were so, He Himself would redeem the souls
from the underworld, if they were to be redeemed (Ps. 49:15;
Job 14:13).

The idea that God ruled over the spirits of man did not
suffice to give satisfaction to those who lived in accordance
with the precepts of the Torah, and yet found themselves
the victims of misfortune. Time and again the Psalmists
complain of their own ill-fortune as against the apparent
good luck of the sinners (Ps. 10:1-15) and other passages. The
pious and the poor apparently suffered while unbelievers
and sinners prospered. One of the finest examples of the
cry of a righteous man, as he doubts the justice of God, is
the Ninety-Fourth Psalm:

O Lord to whom vengeance belongeth,
O Lord to whom vengeance belongeth, shine forth.
Lift up Thyself, Thou judge of the earth;
Render to the proud their recompense.
Lord, how long shall the wicked,
How long shall the wicked exult?

They gush out, they speak arrogancy;
All the workers of iniquity bear themselves loftily,
They crush Thy people, O Lord, and afflict Thy heritage.
They slay the widow and the stranger and murder the
    fatherless.
He that planteth the ear, shall He not hear?
He that formed the eye, shall He not see?
He that instructeth nations, shall not He correct,
Even He that teacheth man knowledge?

Later, the unhappy circumstances under which Israel found itself, did not agree with the promise and the vision of happy days. The promise to Abraham that God will make his progeny a "great people", did not have the implication that it would be a persecuted people. The promise to Moses that He would deliver them "out from under the burdens of Egypt", was not understood as meaning that He would condemn them to the burdens of the Romans. The promise that He would establish "Israel as His people and that He would be their God," at least implied that He would favor them. Thruout the Prophetic and Wisdom literature is the promise found that Israel would be under the special guardianship of God; and this became the very heart of Israel's existence. "The Guardian of Israel neither slumbereth nor sleepeth" (Ps. 121:4) was a firm and fixed conviction in the soul of Israel.

But justice appeared too slow in coming to His people, and the unhappy state of Judea under a change of masters from Assyrian to Babylonian, to Persian to Greek and then to Roman, shook their old belief in the strict justice of God. The messianic hopes of Isaiah and Micah and others, began to be more universally accepted. Still later the continuous absence of a peaceful and quiet existence, and Israel's relations with different peoples with whom they came in contact, and the preachments of the Apocalyptists induced many to change their beliefs. The hope of their salvation lay in the coming of a Messiah who would release them from their troubles.[2] As the messianic hope grew because of the stress of misfortune, so grew also the hope that God will in His own time, take care of His own. But that day seemed too long delayed—and as the woes grew more poignant, the necessity for some kind of faith in the justice of God, became more pressing. That Israel was acquainted with the Persian belief in resurrection, is indicated by the parable of the vision of the valley of dry bones by the Prophet Ezekiel, (37:1-15.) God will blow the breath of life into these dry bones and they will become the House of Israel. Thus saith the Lord God: "Behold, I will open your graves, and cause you to come up out of your graves, O My people; and I will bring you into the land of Israel. And ye shall know that I am the Lord, when I have opened your graves, O My people. And I will put my spirit in you, and ye shall live, and I will place you in your own land; and ye shall know that I the Lord have spoken, and performed it, saith the Lord."

Gradually there developed the belief that the pious will be resurrected, and that their reward will come in the future life. The belief in resurrection held its own for some time, so that there was the insertion in the Prayer Book [3] of a resurrection prayer still included in the Orthodox Prayer Book: "Thou O Lord art mighty forever. Thou revivest the dead. Thou are mighty to save. Thou sustainest the living with loving kindness, revivest the dead with great mercy, supportest the falling, healest the sick, loosest the bound, and keepest thy faith to them that sleep in the dust. Who is like unto Thee, O Lord of mighty acts, and who resembleth Thee O King, who killest and bringest to life and causest salvation to spring forth? Yea, faithful art Thou to revive the dead. Blessed art Thou O Lord, who revivest the dead." This prayer is post-biblical, and dates from the age of the Maccabeans; it indicates a definite departure from biblical conceptions of the after-life. But there is no intimation here that resurrection is a matter of reward, or that non-resurrection is a matter of punishment. The unquestioned acceptance of the resurrection of Jesus by the disciples, was doubtless due to the fact that the belief in resurrection was common among the people of Judea at that time.

Later this idea gave way to the Greek conception of the immortality of the soul. The divine judgment-day was placed in the future, and the decision as to reward or punishment would depend upon the kind of life the individual lived in this world. But it was always stressed that it was God himself who will render the judgments, for His dominion extended over both this world and the hereafter, and there was no need for an intercessor or another redeemer to execute them.

V.

Jewish Concept of Future Life (Continued)

At the time Paul appeared, there was no universal belief in hell or in everlasting punishment among Jews, nor is there generally, now. In the Old Testament, as noted, there is no clear reference to any kind of punishment after this life, and certainly no mention of hell as a place of torture by fire. There are references to extinction by fire of the sinners and sinning nations, but not in the after-world. The two outstanding passages that deal with punishment by fire are found in Isaiah (66:15-16; 24) and read:

"For behold the Lord will come in fire,
    And his chariots shall be like the whirl-wind,
To render His anger with fury
    And His rebuke with flames of fire.
For by fire will the Lord contend
    And by His sword with all flesh.
And the slain of the Lord will be many.
    And they shall go forth and look

* * * * *

Upon the carcasses of the men that rebelled against Me,
    For their worm shall not die
Neither shall their fire be quenched;
    And they shall be an abhorring unto all flesh."

These verses refer to this world where the sinners and the sinning nations would be destroyed. Later however, as indicated, Jewish thought began to postpone the time of punishment. For them it was impossible to doubt the justice of their God in dealing with his loyal followers. If their conduct was not rewarded here, it surely would receive recognition in the future.

The result of this speculation, as well as the influence of later Greek philosophy, encouraged the belief in immortality of the soul. If the righteous failed of reward for their good works in this life, then a just God would see to it that that reward came from Him in the after-life. But the treatment accorded to the soul of the individual was to be a matter for Him and Him alone. As he did not share His glory and His might with someone else, so would He not share His task as the dispenser of justice here or hereafter, nor as the redeemer of those who had sinned, nor as the judge of those who merited forgiveness. This became an inviolate belief of Judaism and has never changed.

The general attitude of the Jew towards any savior or redeemer besides God, has already been dwelt upon in previous pages. Aside from the fact that the idea of an "anointed one" in after-life was not an accepted Jewish teaching, the doctrine that all men were God's children and therefore Jesus could not be His only begotten son, was held true whether for the earthly Jesus or for the Jesus risen. The idea of an unique resurrection of Jesus apart from the resurrection of other dead, was thus incomprehensible to the Jewish mind; and the recognition of the risen Christ as the redeemer thru his blood, was, as we know, foreign to Jewish thinking. Since God alone was the Redeemer, whether in this world or the next, there was no need for the "lamb of sacrifice to atone for the sins of man." (Acts 8:32) And since the Jewish conception of God did not permit of His becoming flesh or taking on any form that was finite, the whole doctrine of the "Lord—that is 'Jesus'—" the only begotten son of God becoming the blood-sacrifice for the sins of men to redeem them from sin and eternal punishment, fell by the wayside. (Col. 1:14-20) and similar verses.

Another important contribution to the impossibility of the Jew's acceptance of Paul's scheme of salvation was that there never was in Judaism, and there is not today, a popular belief in eternal punishment, because it could not be imagined that a just God would punish for eternity, the sins of a mortal whose lease of life was a breath in the passing of time, even though he lived three score and ten or more years. Judaism's conception of the justice of God precluded any dogma that would inflict eternal punishment upon a human being whose span of life was so to speak but an instant. There was never a general belief in Judaism that the soul, even if it went to Gehenna, could not be redeemed. God does reward the good and does punish the evil. But the punishment does not lie in torturing the soul, but rather in preventing the evil soul from sharing in the glory that awaits the righteous. In the framework of such a philosophy there is no room for the Pauline conception that Christ redeems the sinners from the burning fires of eternal damnation. I am stating the general concept of Judaism with regard to reward and punishment in this and in the after-world. There were some deviations. There were apocryphal and apocalyptic writers who did not share these views. But they were in the minority. In the newly revised edition of the Union Prayer Book, there is (p. 109) a quotation from Ben Sirach, an apocryphal writer who lived close to 200 B.C.E., as follows: "Why are earth and ashes proud? When a man is dead, he shall inherit worms."

The general belief about the time of Paul and sometime after, was that the righteous would inherit eternal bliss in the world to come, while the wicked "hovered"[1] over the horizon of the earth as restless demoniacal spirits, finally to succumb to the fate of annihilation, after they had been cast down into the fiery pit of Gehenna or Sheol." But these would nevertheless get an opportunity to be tried by a twelve month test of purification by the fires of Gehenna, and after that they would be transplanted to Paradise, if God willed, where rested the souls of the righteous. Every man had the privilege of living a righteous life and inheriting Paradise, or of living a wicked life and going to purgatory, knowing that after a term of purification, he too would spend eternity among the righteous if he merited this. Another belief current at this time differed from the above. It taught that God would forgive those who earned forgiveness while the unregenerate would remain in purgatory, punished only to the extent of not being able to bask in the glory of God in Paradise. Since, under the Jewish tradition man was not born under the sin of Adam, he could thru the prayers of a son or thru the merits of his fathers, attain that purity which would entitle him to Paradise, without needing someone else to atone for his sins. The whole Pauline system of the crucifixion of Jesus, so that by his sacrifice he "might deliver us from this present evil world and redeem us from the punishment brought on by the sin of Adam" as (Col. 1:14) has it: "He (God) hath delivered us from the power of darkness . . . and hath translated us into the kingdom of his dear son in whom we have redemption thru his blood even the forgiveness of sins," was not accepted by ancient Israel, and is not accepted by contemporary Judaism.

Concurrent with the belief in the resurrection of the body there was also the belief among some, that souls of the pious go to heaven, there dwelling around the throne of the Almighty, until the world is again renewed. Many opposed this belief, maintaining that the burning of souls in Gehenna was contrary to the very conception of the soul, since it is of purely spiritual and divine nature. In rabbinic times, we find the following conception which was being developed previous to, during, and soon after New Testament times: Rabbi Jochanan[2] taught: "All promises held forth in Scripture in definite form, refer to the Messianic era. In regard to the bliss awaiting the pious in the world to come, the words of the Prophet Isaiah hold true: "No eye hath seen it, O God, beside Thee." Rab[3] said: "In the world to come there are no sensual enjoyments nor passions; there is no eating or drinking; and no marrying and giving in marriage, but the righteous sit with crowns on their heads, basking in the splendor of Divine glory." Rabbi Simeon ben Lakish went even so far as to say, "there is neither hell nor paradise. Instead, God sends out the sun in its full strength from its encasement, and the wicked are consumed by its heat, while the pious find delight and healing in its beams."

A very old teaching the date of whose origin I cannot determine is: "To the righteous of all nations, there is a portion in the world to come." This teaching is accepted by most of those who profess Judaism today.

In the Authorized Daily Prayer Book, Revised Edition, by Dr. Joseph H. Hertz, late Chief Rabbi of the British Empire, (p. 255), we find the following statement: "Many and various are the folk-beliefs and poetic fancies concerning Heaven, (Gan Eden), and Hell, (Gehinnom). Our most authoritative religious guides, however, proclaim that "no eye hath seen, nor can mortal fathom, what awaiteth us in the hereafter; but that even the tarnished soul will not forever be denied spiritual bliss." Judaism rejects the doctrine of eternal damnation, according to this scholar, "The pious since Maccabean times," he says, "have believed not only in the soul's survival of death and decay, but that in God's unfathomable wisdom and in his own time, the body will be reunited with the soul. Maimonides and Yahudah Hallevi make the doctrine of the revival of the dead, identical with that of the immortality of the soul, and explain the Talmudic sayings to the contrary as figurative language."

Some of these Talmudic sayings are included in the famous "Aboth" or "Sayings of the Fathers," reprinted in the traditional Authorized Daily Prayer Book. It is one of the Tractates of the Mishna and is a body of wise and edifying moral maxims and teachings, that to a surprising extent molded the character of post-rabbinic Jews. Even today, the reader will find light and inspiration in them in the sphere of moral conduct. There is frequent use of the expression "a share in the world to come," but no explanation of the meaning of the phrase. Said Akabya the son of Mahalalel (contemporary of Hillel): "Reflect upon three things, and thou wilt not come within the power of sin: know whence thou comest, whither thou art going, and before Whom thou wilt in future have to give account and reckoning. Whence thou comest— from a fetid drop; whither thou art going—to a place of dust, worms and maggots; and before Whom thou wilt in future have to give account and reckoning — before the Supreme King of kings, the Holy One blessed be He." (Beginning Ch. 3).

Rabbi Levitas of Jabneh, a contemporary of Rabbi Akiba (circa 50-132) said: "Be exceedingly lowly of spirit, since the hope of man is but a worm." (Ch. 4). Rabbi Elazar HaKappar a contemporary of Judah the Prince (150-220), used to say: "They that are born are destined to die; and the dead to be brought to life again; . . . know also that everything is according to the reckoning; let not thy imagination give thee hope that the grave will be a place of refuge for thee; . . . perforce thou wilt in the future have to give account and reckoning before the Supreme King of kings, the Holy One, blessed be He." (Ch. 4). One unnamed rabbi did not reject the doctrine of eternal damnation, at least not for non-Jews, in this case perhaps the progenitor of that religion that used to maintain that there is no salvation outside that particular church. He said: "The disciples of Abraham

143

our father, enjoy this world and inherit the world to come; the disciples of Baalam the wicked, inherit Gehinnom and descend into the pit of destruction," quoting Psalm (55:24). "But Thou O God, wilt bring them down into the nether most pit."

For many centuries the most generally accepted doctrine of life after death, was that of the resurrection of the dead. Orthodox Jewry still recites the prayer which says "Blessed art Thou who causest the dead to live" or as another translation goes, "Blessed art Thou who restorest souls into dead bodies." (Singer-Abrahams Daily Prayer Book, p. 5, 45) Many Orthodox Jews profess to believe in it now. But it must be emphasized that so far as we now know, there was no unanimous acceptance of any one belief about life after death,[4] after the destruction of the first Temple. But there was complete rejection of any role played by Christ, according to Pauline teaching. Immortality of the soul is also nowhere taught in the Old Testament; it became a popular belief under Hellenistic influence, as noted.

To sum up the Biblical and post-Biblical beliefs in reward and punishment after death, we can make this general statement, because there was no complete unanimity: The Bible says nothing about punishment after death. The shades of the dead live in a world of subterranean shadows, without reference to reward or punishment. Late biblical and post-biblical Judaism began to develop the idea of resurrection of the dead, in which the pious souls enjoyed bliss in Paradise until the coming of the Messiah when souls and bodies would be joined together to live in eternal happiness. The other souls would go to purgatory or Gehenna, there to be held for a year of purification; or if they were not purified, they might in time be either annihilated in the fires of Gehenna or remain in shame and everlasting contempt. God alone was to be the redeemer of souls and determine their fate. Prayers were efficacious and could help to redeem the sinful according to some. The more accepted was the belief that sinful unredeemed souls just melt away, without torture and without punishment. It is enough that they are denied the bliss of heaven. Punishment of the soul was later objected to because of the concept of materiality involved in the word "punishment," whereas the soul is a spiritual entity.

None of the various Jewish concepts of the future life and the part God plays in them, fits the Pauline scheme of salvation. By the ancient Jews, Paul's teachings were regarded as non-Jewish and anti-Jewish doctrines and thus found no acceptance; and this is the position of the modern Jew.

VI.

Paul's Attitude Toward the Law (Torah)

Paul's attitude toward the "Law" or "Torah" or the "Teaching," was very distasteful to his Jewish contemporaries. The word "Torah" was first applied to the Five Books of Moses; then to the entire Scripture, and later was used to designate the whole body of Jewish tradition. Judaism's most holy possession in olden days and today is the Torah, commonly translated, but wrongly, as the "Law." It has never lost its sanctity and tho there may be different interpretations of its passages, as a symbol of Israel's existence and destiny, it has always retained the highest place. To belittle it and cast it off, was regarded as a major sin. As the doctrine of the supremacy of the risen Messiah progressed, the sanctity of the Torah was lessened in the eyes of Paul. Somehow he could not understand that the preservation of the Torah by Israel was the only guarantee of its selection as the "chosen people," as God's "own treasure" and is its charter to be man's religious teacher as God's "first-born." It was the pivot about which the life of the individual Jew and the nation, revolved. It was the Book of Instruction for the whole people —it was the very heart of its spiritual and material existence. It is the guiding plan from which the world was created— "it is Truth itself." [1] A non-Jew can hardly realize how deep the affection for the Torah is, with what reverence it is regarded, and with what loyalty it has been defended. In the use of the word "Torah" here, I refer to the Pentateuch or the Five Books of Moses, which have always, even since the closing of the canon, formed one holy collection, and have been revered as the most important part of the Old Testament.

It must not be forgotten that at the time of Paul, the other parts of what is now the Old Testament were not even permitted in the same scroll as the Torah. The Torah was God's revelation to Moses at Sinai and was uniquely divine.

It was the blue-print of the Supreme Architect, for the world. It was given at Mt. Sinai but was to be tranmitted to succeeding generations. For the Jews of yesterday, and for the Jews of today, the words of (Dt. 29:9ff) still have meaning: "Ye are standing here this day, all of you before the Lord your God . . . that thou shouldst enter into the convenant of the Lord thy God . . . which the Lord thy God maketh with you this day; that He may establish thee this day unto Himself as a people, and that He may be unto thee a God, as he spoke unto thee, and as he swore unto thy fathers, Abraham, Isaac and Jacob. Neither with you only do I make this convenant. . . . But also with him that is not here with us this day." That is to say, this convenant was made with the unborn generations that will spring from the loins of Israel. The whole tradition of Israel's history, its origin, its spiritual heritage, its source of knowledge of its Creator and Father, its very life, are founded upon and buttressed by the Torah!

To utter the new teaching as Paul did (Gal. 2:16), that "a man is not justified by the works of the Law, but by the faith of Jesus Christ . . . that we might be justified by the faith of Jesus Christ, and not by the works of the Law; for by the works of the Law shall no flesh be justified," is to tear down the whole foundation of Jewish existence, its belief and future. To say: "no one is pronounced 'acquitted' by doing what the Torah requires and "everyone is considered 'acquitted' by his faith in Christ," is simply throwing the Torah out of the window! Paul did just this. There are several statements particularly in Galatians in which Paul

147

repudiates the Torah. The Jews, of course, not only did not accept this Pauline view, but resented it. To quote Prof. Riddle: [2] "Paul's Jewish contemporaries immediately perceived that these conceptions were as antithetical to Judaism as opposites could be." Whether Paul was not able to see that these teachings separated him from the whole House of Israel, one cannot know. But it would seem that he would know that the violation of circumcision and dietary laws marked a definite break between those who observed these and other laws and those who did not. Perhaps he did not care!

It is not possible to believe that Paul did not know that the carrying out of the precepts of the Torah—the Law—"acquitted" the individual Jew. About that there was never any question. Judaism acknowledged the belief that man was created with an evil as well as a good nature, but God gave Israel the Torah, which was the instrument by which the evil inclination was subdued and overcome. The Jew was taught that from the beginning, God said in speaking of Abraham (Gen. 18:19), "for I have known him to the end that he may command his children and his household after him. That they may keep the way of the Lord, to do righteousness and justice." If they did this, God, would multiply them and not punish them. Israel's election was recorded in the Torah: (Ex. 19:5-6) "Now therefore, if ye will hearken unto My voice indeed, and keep My covenant, then ye shall be Mine own treasure from among all peoples . . . ye shall be unto Me a kingdom of priests and a holy nation," and in a number of passages of similar import.

To the Jew, the Torah meant life. (Lev. 18:5) "Mine ordinances shall ye do and My statutes shall ye keep to walk therein . . . which if a man do, he shall live by them. I am the Lord." But to Paul, it meant spiritual death. It faded out for him when the risen Christ idea was developed by him. He had evolved the curious concept that the Torah demanded full and complete compliance with the 613 positive and negative commandments in it. There was never such a belief. The soul that sinned could be redeemed even if some commandments were violated. Individual redemption was a part of God's mercy, for He is indeed "merciful, gracious, and long-suffering . . . forgiving iniquity, transgression and sin" (Ex. 34:7) and similar passages. He was wrong in thinking that those who failed to observe all of them were doomed to eternal death. Brooding on this idea, he found that he had been too sinful to observe them all, and sought salvation by faith in Christ. The abrogation of that which was dearest to his fellow Hebrews, which cemented them together, which gave them purpose, support, hope and love of their Creator, alienated his former coreligionists—coreligionists no longer. For if ever there was a people united by a common religious tradition that held them together, it was and is, Israel. Without the Torah, there was no Israel, no Chosen People, no Holy Nation, and no worshipper of God in the Jewish sense. For Paul, Christ was the exemplar; Paul substituted the Chosen "One," for the Chosen "People"; for him the Torah was a hindrance and a stumbling block for it was only the "law of the spirit in Christ that freed him." (Ro. 8:2).

149

Contrast the attitude of Paul towards the Torah with that of the blessings which are recited before and after reading it at least once a week, since time immemorial: "Blessed art Thou O God, King of the Universe, who hast chosen us from all people, and hast given us Thy Torah. Blessed art Thou O God, Giver of the Torah." "Blessed art Thou O God, King of the Universe, who hast given us the Law of Truth, and hast planted everlasting life in our midst. Blessed art Thou, O Lord, Giver of the Torah." Contrast with Paul's attitude, also, the more than 2000 year-old apostrophe from the Book of Proverbs (3:18-19), applied in the ritual to the reading of the Holy Torah, recited on every occasion on which it is read: "The Torah is a tree of life to those who lay hold of it and the supporters thereof are happy; its ways are ways of pleasantness and all its paths lead to peace."[3] This has always been—and is now—the historical attitude of Jews towards their precious inheritance, the Torah, which has become a symbol of the faith, as well as of the mission and the destiny of the House of Israel.

It is not possible for a Jew to conceive that he was or is under a curse because he is "under the Law"—the Torah. Equally inconceivable to the Jew was it that "Christ hath redeemed us from the curse of the Law, being made a curse for us." (Gal. 3:13.) If this is an original Pauline statement, it shows how completely estranged Paul had become from the stream of Jewish tradition. An assertion like this could be made to the Gentile Christians, but never to professing Jews, particularly to the Judeans, whose greatest joy was to "bear the yoke of the Torah."

150

If Paul really studied under Gamaliel the eminent teacher and head of the Sanhedrin, and there is considerable doubt about this; if he were in reality a "Hebrew of the Hebrews," and if he were a sincere Pharisee, he surely would have known that the Jews bore the "Yoke of the Torah" gladly. He would have known that this holy, eternal, divine instrument of God's revelation was the hallmark of their election. For the Holy Torah, Israel lived then, and withholds no sacrifice now. One can believe only that if Paul actually told his listeners to reject the Torah, he must have done it late in life, after withdrawing himself from the most sacred traditions of the Jewish people and forsaking them completely!

While Jesus of Nazareth is the central character of the Christian religion, Paul is without doubt the founder of Christianity as we know it. Thruout these nineteen centuries, the main direction of Pauline teachings has been followed. There is no doubt in my mind and in the minds of many others, that had it not been for Paul and the churches and followers he created, Christianity could never have become the dominant western religion. Whether Judaism or Mithraism or one of the other mystery religions would have spread over the western world, one cannot say. Suffice it to observe, that it was Paul who stopped the spread of Judaism, by creating and projecting a religion that better and more easily met the conditions of chaos and change which faced him and his time, and better fitted the various religious concepts that abounded.

The Dead Sea Scrolls

Towards the end of the Spring of 1947, an Arab accidentally discovered a cave on the western side of the northern section of the Dead Sea, which contained a number of ancient scrolls. These turned out to be the remaining records of a library which appeared to be the center of a colony of Essenes. The scrolls are written in Hebrew, and thus far an invaluable treasury of ancient knowledge has come into the possession of Biblical scholars.

This literature, it is now pretty well agreed, is the product of the Essenes, a Jewish sect mentioned by Josephus and Philo as being one of the three main sects of Israel. Some New Testament scholars maintained that Jesus belonged to the Essene sect, but this position was not generally accepted. Now, the translation of many of these scrolls indicates that there was a very close relationship between the Essenes and the pre-Christian and early Christian teachings, and between Essenic Judaism and the beginnings of Christianity.

This is not the place to go into a discussion of the Dead Sea Scrolls. The fact that there was a similarity between the teachings of the Essenes and those of the New Testament, in no way affects the discussions in this book. These are based upon the present text of the New Testament and have nothing to do with the Dead Sea Scrolls. Prof. Dupont-Sommer of Paris has published his own investigation of The Dead Sea Scrolls, which shows close relationship between some of their content and the New Testament. To his work I refer those who are interested in further exploring the extraordinary resemblance of the teachings of these two ancient groups. I mention the Dead Sea Scrolls here because of the wide interest they have elicited, and because I want it understood that the exposition of the teachings of Jesus and Paul were judged solely on the basis of the present text of the New Testament.

Finis

NOTES

PART I.

SECTION I.

1. Shirley Jackson Case, The Historicity of Jesus, Ch. 1.
2. Joseph Klausner, Jesus of Nazareth, p. 19ff.
   H. Graetz, History of the Jews, Vol. II, p. 168.
3. Solomon Zeitlin, Who Crucified Jesus? p. 37ff.
4. Graetz, idem, Vol. II, p. 62ff.
5. Josephus, Antiquities, Bk. XIV, Ch. 16; Bk. XVII, Ch. 10.
6. Zeitlin, idem, Ch. III, Sec. II.
7. Graetz, idem, Vol. II, p. 137ff.
8. A. H. Silver, Messianic Speculations in Ancient Israel.
   Article Pseudo-Messiahs, Jewish Encyclopedia, Vol. X, p. 251.
   S. Schechter, Studies in Judaism, p. 224.
9. Zeitlin, idem, p. 53ff.
10. Emil Schurer, The Jewish People in the Time of Jesus Christ, 1st Div., Vol. II, Sec. 17.

SECTION II.

1. D. F. Strauss, Life of Jesus, 4th Ed., p. 117ff.
2. Case, Historicity, p. 136.
3. Case, idem, p. 25ff; 142-143.
4. R. H. Charles, Eschatology, pp. 359-360.
5. A. T. Olmstead, Jesus, p. 46.
6. Case, idem, pp. 147-148.
7. Schurer, The Jewish People in the Time of Jesus Christ, idem, pp. 182-3.
8. K. Kohler, Jewish Theology, Ch. LIII.
9. It should be noted here that there is one school of New Testament students that maintains that Jesus never regarded himself as the Messiah, and another that does not believe that the Jesus of the Gospels ever lived.

SECTION III.

1. Josephus, Antiquities, Bk. 17, Ch. 10.
   Graetz, History, Vol. II, Chs. 5, 8, 12.
2. Jew. Encyclopedia, Vol. X, p. 251.

3. Donald W. Riddle, Early Christian Life, Chs. 5-6.

4. G. F. Moore, Judaism, Vol. I, Ch. 6.

5. Case, Historicity, p. 136.

SECTION IV.

1. Riddle and Hutson, New Testament Life and Literature, p. 156ff.

2. Casper Rene Gregory, Canon and Text of the New Testament, p. 44.

3. James Moffat, Introduction to the Literature of the New Testament, p. 1.

4. Chas. Guignebert, Christianity, Intro. and p. 21ff.

5. Case, Historicity, p. 136ff; 210.

6. Graetz, History, Vol. II, Ch. 6.

7. Moore, Judaism, Vol. I, Ch. 7.

8. James Parkes, The Conflict of the Church and the Synagog, Intro. p. XVIII.

9. S. M. Lindo, History of the Jews of Spain and Portugal, p. 10.

10. Margolis & Marx, History of the Jewish People, p. 304.

11. Graetz, idem, Vol. II, p. 563ff.

12. Jewish Encyclopedia, Vol. IV, p, 614.

13. Consult any history of the Spanish and Portuguese Jews or the Spanish Inquisition. The sufferings inflicted by the Church were similar in most of the European nations as well as in South America and Mexico.

SECTION V.

1. G. George Fox, Judaism, Christianity and the Modern Social Ideals, pp. 248-249.

2. Kohler, Theology, pp. 88-89; 288ff.

3. M. Friedlander, The Jewish Religion, p. 38ff.

4. Union Prayer Book, Newly Revised, Atonement Day Services.

SECTION VI.

1. Klausner, Jesus of Nazareth, pp. 94-95.

2. Case, Historicity, p. 283.

3. James Parkes, Judaism and Christianity, p. 41.

SECTION VII.

1. Klausner, Jesus of Nazareth, p. 363. Julius Wellhausen was one of the most outstanding Christian theologians of his day. He was a German Protestant.

2. Case, Historicity of Jesus; Evolution of Christianity.

3. Talmud Shabbat, 31a.

SECTION VIII.

1. Talmud Shabbat, 31a.
2. Sifra to Leviticus, 19:34.
3. Abrahams-Singer, Daily Prayer Book, pp. 234, 264.

PART II.

SECTION I.

1. Mt. 16:13-20; Mk. 8:27-30; Lk. 9:18-21.
2. Mt. 20:29-34; Mk. 10:46-52; Lk. 18:35-43.
3. Mt. 21:1-11; Mk. 11:1-11; Lk. 19:29-44; Jn. 12:12-19.
4. Mt. 17:5-9; Mk. 9:7; Lk. 9:34-35.
5. Mt. 9:6; Mk. 2:5; Lk. 5:24.
6. Mt. 16:28; Mk. 9:1; Lk. 9:27.
7. Mt. 21:1-11; Mk. 11:1-11; Lk. 19:29-34; Jn. 12:12-19.
8. The Passover, the Feast of Weeks and the Feast of Tabernacles were called the Pilgrim Festivals because during them pilgrimages were made to the Temple whenever possible.
9. Klausner, Jesus of Nazareth, p. 313ff, where Talmudic sources are given.

SECTION II.

1. Zeitlin, Who Crucified Jesus? Ch. X.
2. Parkes, Judaism and Christianity, pp. 66-69.
3. Klausner, Jesus of Nazareth, pp. 336ff; Riddle & Hutson, New Testament Life and Literature, p. 66.
4. Mt. 27:11-14; Mk. 15:2-5; Lk. 23:3.

SECTION IV.

1. Cf. Mt. 26:47; Mk. 14:43; Lk. 22:47.

PART III.

SECTION I.

1. Riddle, Early Christian Life, Chs. I-III.
2. A. C. Barnett, The New Testament, Its Making and Meaning, p. 94ff.
3. T. R. Glover, Paul of Tarsus, p. 68.

SECTION II.

1. Case, Evolution of Early Christianity, Ch. IV.
2. F. Cumont, Oriental Religions in Roman Paganism, Pref. XXII; p. 103ff.
3. J. G. Frazer, Golden Bough, Vol. I, p. 300.
   W. O. E. Oesterley, Judaism and Christianity, Ch. VII.
   Case, Historicity, p. 141ff.
   Riddle, Early Christian Life, p. 55.
4. Riddle, Paul, Man of Conflict, p. 37.
5. Case, Evolution of Christianity, p. 353.
6. Case, idem, 112.
7. Glover, Paul of Tarsus, p. 59.
8. Case, idem, pp. 314, 329.
9. Riddle, idem, p. 152.
10. Jew. Encyclopedia, Vol. XI, p. 79ff.

SECTION III.

1. J. Weiss, Paul and Jesus, p. 4.
2. M. Friedlander, The Jewish Religion, pp. 38-43.
3. It is obvious that God cannot stand in any relation to time and space. Maimonides, Guide to the Perplexed, Book I, Ch. 52.
4. Nicene and Apostles' Creeds.
5. Riddle, Paul, Man of Conflict, p. 162.
6. Cf. Maimonides, idem, Ch. 35.
7. Anthropomorphism is the ascribing of human form or attributes to beings or things not human, especially Deity.
8. Case, Evolution, pp. 157, 113.
9. Riddle and Hutson, New Testament Life and Literature, p. 107.
10. Glover, Paul of Tarsus, p. 96.

SECTION IV.

1. Kohler, Jewish Theology, p. 281.
2. J. Drummond, The Jewish Messiah, Chs. XIII and XXIV.
3. Authorized Daily Prayer Book, p. 44.

SECTION V.

1. Kohler, Theology, Chs. XLIII-XLIV.
2. Kohler, idem, p. 306ff.
3. Talmud, Berachoth 17a.
4. S. Schechter, Studies in Judaism, pp. 213-214.

SECTION VI.

1. S. Schechter, Some Aspects of Rabbinic Theology, Ch. IX, "Joy of the Law."
2. Riddle, Paul, Man of Conflict, p. 148.
3. Proverbs, 3:17-18. Cf. Hertz, Authorized Daily Prayer Book, p. 492.